CW01656084

O[illegible]
Comprehension

Formerly 'Once a Week'

BOOK THREE

By HAYDN PERRY

Diploma in English Literature, University of London
formerly Headmaster, Merryhills School, Enfield

GINN AND COMPANY LTD

© Haydn Perry 1960

Without Answers
Thirty-fifth impression 1995 039511
ISBN 0 602 29712 6

With Answers
Sixteenth impression 1995 019505
ISBN 0 602 22422 5

Published by Ginn and Company Ltd
Prebendal House, Parson's Fee
Aylesbury, Bucks HP20 2QY

Printed in Great Britain by
Henry Ling Ltd, Dorchester, Dorset

PREFACE

This book of English tests is intended for fourth-year pupils of Primary Schools. It can be used either for testing progress and ability, or it can serve as a textbook from which pupils can work alone or with the teacher's help.

In each of the thirty tests, the first question is of the comprehension type. These questions test the reading and reasoning of the pupils. More than sixty other types of questions are included in these books. All branches of English suitable for the age-group are thus adequately tested.

TO THE PUPIL

In each of the thirty tests there are five questions.

Read each question carefully, so that you understand exactly what you are asked to do before you begin.

Do not spend too long on any one question. You should answer all five questions in 45 minutes.

Make sure that you have not missed a question, or part of one.

If you find that you have made a mistake, alter your work clearly and neatly so that your teacher will know what it is you mean him to read and mark.

HAYDN PERRY

TEST 1

I. Read very carefully through the following passage, and then answer the questions.

Jason's Task

The gates were opened and the magic bulls leaped out. Their brazen hoofs rang upon the ground, their nostrils sent out sheets of flame, and they rushed with lowered heads upon Jason. He flinched never a step. The flame of their breath swept around him, but it singed not a hair of his head; and the bulls stopped short, and trembled.

Then Jason sprang upon the nearest and seized him by the horns; and up and down they wrestled until the bull fell grovelling on his knees; for the heat of the brute died within him, and his mighty limbs were loosed.

So both the bulls were tamed and yoked; and Jason bound them to the plough, and goaded them onward with his lance till he had ploughed the sacred field. Then he took the serpents' teeth and sowed them, and waited what would befall.

Charles Kingsley

1. What happened when the gates were opened?
2. How many animals were there?
3. What was strange about their breath?
4. What did the animals do when they saw Jason?
5. Write the sentence which tells us that Jason was unafraid.
6. With which bull did Jason wrestle?
7. What work did Jason force the bulls to do?
8. What did he use instead of a whip?
9. What did Jason sow in the ground?
10. What words or phrases in the story mean (*a*) scorched; (*b*) forced them onward; (*c*) holy; (*d*) waited to see what would happen?
11. From this list, choose words that describe the events that took place: extraordinary, magical, usual, commonplace, remarkable, notable, eventful, moderate, impressive, fantastic.

12. Which of the following would make a suitable title for the extract: (*a*) At the Spanish Bullfight. (*b*) Taken from a Greek Myth. (*c*) A Peaceful Rural Encounter?

II. When we wish to say that someone is **blind,** we may say **as blind as a bat.**

Choose the correct answers from these:

1. As brave as (*a*) a soldier; (*b*) a sailor; (*c*) a lion.
2. As cunning as (*a*) a flea; (*b*) a fox; (*c*) a miser.
3. As stubborn as (*a*) a mule; (*b*) a hen; (*c*) a bull.
4. As sure-footed as (*a*) a hiker; (*b*) a mountain-goat; (*c*) a toddler.
5. As brown as (*a*) a biscuit; (*b*) a banana; (*c*) a berry.
6. As timid as (*a*) a horse; (*b*) a mouse; (*c*) a moose.

III. Here are two words, **arm** and **chair.** From these we can make the compound word **arm-chair.**

Make six new compound words from the following:

hedge	bone	sea	sparrow
flower	deck	collar	tooth
chest	bed	brush	quarter

IV. When speaking of a number of people, we may use the word **crowd.** What words might we use when speaking of:

1. People at a football match.
2. People at a concert.
3. People in a church.
4. People in a riot.

V. Rewrite these sentences in the **plural** form.

Example: The **boy** climbed the **tree.** The **boys** climbed the **trees.**

1. I saw the banjo on the table.
2. The baby opened the box.
3. My brother-in-law served as a fighter-pilot.
4. The girl chased the thief.
5. The hunter fired on the wolf.
6. The salmon and the trout swam safely away.

TEST 2

I. Read very carefully through the following passage, and then answer the questions.

Aboard the 'Hispaniola'

It was such a scene of confusion as you can hardly fancy. All the lockfast places had been broken open in quest of the chart. The floor was thick with mud, where ruffians had sat down to drink or consult after wading in the marshes round their camp. The bulkheads, all painted in clear white and beaded round with gilt, bore a pattern of dirty hands. Dozens of empty bottles clinked together to the rolling of the ship. One of the doctor's medical books lay open on the table, half of the leaves gutted out for pipelights. The lamp still cast a smoky glow, obscure and brown as amber.

I went into the cellar; all the barrels were gone, and of the bottles a most surprising number had been drunk out and thrown away. Since the mutiny began, not a man of them could have been sober.

R. L. Stevenson

1. For what had the ruffians been searching?
2. Where had the mud come from that covered the floor?
3. How had the bulkheads been decorated when the ship was built?
4. With what were the bulkheads now soiled?
5. Pages had been torn from the book. For what reason?
6. How can we tell that not a great deal of time had passed since the ruffians left the ship?
7. What was usually stored in the cellar?
8. What made the bottles clink together?
9. What words or phrases in the story mean (*a*) cupboards; (*b*) wild fellows; (*c*) in search of; (*d*) have a discussion; (*e*) torn out?
10. From this list, choose words that describe the scene in the cellar: comely, attractive, slimy, unkempt, foul, elegant, offensive, confused, spotless, beastly, unattractive, unsoiled.

11. What name is given to 'people who take part in a mutiny'?
12. Which of these titles describes what you have read: (*a*) Ship-shape and Bristol Fashion. (*b*) Inconsiderate Visitors to a Vessel. (*c*) All in Apple-pie Order?
13. Write the **opposites** of these words that are used in the passage: sober, dirty, open, began.

II. There are errors in each of the following sentences. Rewrite the sentences correctly.

1. Me and him are going to the football match.
2. Who is the cleverest now, Tom nor Harry?
3. It is a pity that the footballer has broke his leg.
4. Give him them books to read.

III. Rewrite these sentences using one word instead of the phrases in heavy type:

1. The ship sank, leaving much **wreckage floating on the surface.**
2. The rescuers found few **people still alive.**
3. One man managed to swim into the **calm water beyond the coral reef.**
4. Then he climbed to the **highest point** of the hill.
5. From here he could see the **complete view in all directions.**
6. He **made up his mind** to cross to the other side of the island.

IV. Rewrite these sentences using the **opposite** of the word in heavy type to fill each space.

1. The car was **moving,** but the lorry was ——.
2. Glass is **transparent,** but brick is ——.
3. The balloon **expands** when warm, but —— when cold.
4. You seem to want the **maximum** pay for the —— work.

V. Write these twelve names in **alphabetical order:**

Adams	Duncan	Browning	Brown
Chivers	Andrews	Bruce	Clarke
Atkins	Davies	Clark	Davis

TEST 3

I. Read very carefully through the following passage, and then answer the questions.

Gulliver at Dinner

The queen became so fond of my company that she could not dine without me. I had a table placed upon that at which she ate, just at her left elbow, and a chair to sit on. Glumdalclitch stood on a stool near my table to assist and to take care of me. I had an entire set of silver dishes and plates, and other necessaries, which, in proportion to those of the queen's, were not much bigger than those I have seen of the same kind in a London toy-shop, for a baby-house. These my nurse kept in her pocket in a silver box, and gave me at meals as I wanted them, always cleaning them herself. No person dined with the queen save the two princesses royal, the elder sixteen years old, and the younger at that time thirteen and a month.

Jonathan Swift

1. How do we know that the queen was fond of Gulliver?
2. Where was Gulliver's table placed?
3. What did he have for his own use?
4. Where were the dishes kept when they were not in use?
5. Whose duty was it to keep these things clean?
6. Name **all** the people who were present at meals.
7. How old were the queen's daughters at the time of the story?
8. What are the daughters called in the story?
9. What words or phrases in the story have these meanings: (*a*) complete; (*b*) things that are needed; (*c*) compared with; (*d*) except for?
10. From these words make two lists, the first describing the queen and the second describing Gulliver: gigantic, enormous, dwarfish, tremendous, tiny, diminutive, pygmy, large, Brobdingnagian, lusty, vast, little, towering, mountainous, lofty.
11. Read through these statements, and then decide whether each is **true, untrue,** or **cannot be proved:** (*a*) The queen was a

vegetarian. (*b*) Gulliver was the queen's favourite. (*c*) Glumdalclitch was a female. (*d*) Many people were present for dinner. (*e*) The queen had two children only. (*f*) Gulliver had never been to London.

II. Write in full the **abbreviations** shown in heavy type in these sentences:

1. My father can get **B.B.C.** and **I.T.A.** programmes on his television set, but not **V.H.F.** on his radio.
2. Mr. Smith flew on **B.A.**, and Mr. Jones on **T.W.A.**
3. **Det. Insp.** Jones of the **C.I.D.** was handling the case.
4. **A.B.** Jones of **H.M.S.** Evergallant won the **V.C.**

III. We call **up and down** a word-double. Complete these sentences with the correct word-doubles:

1. The thief was soon under **lock and** ——.
2. They fought **hammer and** —— to avoid arrest.
3. It was **touch and** ——
4. They were caught **fair and** ——.

IV. Here are five sentences from a paragraph, but they are not in their correct order. Rewrite them in the order in which they should appear:

1. Only then could he see the destruction his enemies had wrought.
2. At last he found it and pressed it down.
3. Alan groped his way, trying to find the switch.
4. He was almost ready to weep in the darkness.
5. The room was instantly flooded with light.

V. In the following sentences, change all the **masculine** words into **feminine** words.

Example: The **giant** towered over my **father.** The **giantess** towered over my **mother.**

1. He gave him the fox for a present.
2. The hunter chased the stag.
3. The shepherd rode after his flock on a stallion.
4. My father-in-law is an earl.

TEST 4

I. Read very carefully through the following passage, and then answer the questions.

Up the River

The vegetation on the banks had crept closer and closer, shutting out the view. Tall trees leaned forward as if they wished to shake tops with their neighbours on the other side of the river. The only noises were the monotonous chug-chug of the launch and the conversations of the natives who squatted idly in the canoes.

The river narrowed, and the current flowed more swiftly. The bushes seemed more impenetrable than ever, the branches overhead denser. In the distance a faint booming could be heard. Then the launch swung round a bend—and there were the falls. Everyone gazed spellbound at the beautiful cascade which was at least one hundred and fifty feet high. The air was cloudy with spray, and as the sun shone on the vapour it seemed as if a rainbow had suddenly come to life.

1. How do we know that the trees were not upright?
2. Write down the two phrases that might make you think the trees and bushes were human beings.
3. What were the only noises heard at first?
4. Why was the chugging of the engine **monotonous?**
5. When did the party get their first sight of the falls?
6. What caused the booming sound?
7. What made it seem as if they were looking at a rainbow?
8. What made the air cloudy with spray?
9. What words or phrases in the story mean (*a*) extremely difficult to pass through; (*b*) waterfall; (*c*) those living near one another; (*d*) trees and bushes?
10. Complete these words, which are similar in meaning to **spellbound:**

    (*a*) fasc ------ (*b*) hyp------- (*c*) aston-----
    (*d*) ama--- (*e*) astou---- (*f*) stup-----
    (*g*) petr----- (*h*) dumb-------

11. Which of these statements are correct: (*a*) The natives were always silent. (*b*) After a time, the river became much narrower. (*c*) The falls were in view for a very long time. (*d*) A most beautiful sight met their eyes?

II. **Punctuation marks** and **capital letters** have been omitted from the following sentences. Rewrite the sentences correctly:

1. the rocket red in colour soared into the air
2. there is a ship on the reef exclaimed paul
3. is she in great danger the stranger asked
4. shell hold but dont be too long was the reply

III. **Odd man out.** In each of the following groups of words, one is out of place because it has nothing to do with the other four. Write down the odd word.

1. boy, girl, man, beautiful, woman
2. tulip, daffodil, pansy, narcissus, crocus
3. here, there, nowhere, everywhere, somewhere
4. seeing, hearing, tasting, touching, waiting
5. pretty, hasty, nasty, comely, ugly
6. wise, tall, short, big, small

IV. **This** is to **that.** Complete the following sentences.

Example: **Man** is to **woman** as **boy** is to ——. The missing word is **girl.**

1. **Monday** is to **Tuesday** as **Friday** is to ——.
2. **Fact** is to **fiction** as **true** is to ——.
3. **Ball** is to **hockey** as —— is to **ice-hockey.**
4. **Chick** is to **egg** as **butterfly** is to ——.
5. **Palace** is to **king** as **igloo** is to ——.

V. Here are some **crossword-puzzle clues,** and parts of each answer. Write the words in full.

1. Opposite to the floor.	C--LING
2. Cattle graze in this.	F--LD
3. We write with this.	PEN-IL
4. We eat this for breakfast.	-ER-AL
5. Often found in a cake.	C-RR-NT
6. Thankful.	GR---FUL

TEST 5

I. Read very carefully through the following verses, and then answer the questions.

The Lincolnshire Poacher

When I was bound apprentice in famous Lincolnshire,
Full well I served my master for more than seven year,
Till I took up poaching—as you shall quickly hear:
  Oh 'tis my delight on a shiny night,
  In the season of the year!

As me and my comrade were setting of a snare,
'Twas then we spied the gamekeeper, for him we did not care,
For we can wrestle and fight, my boys, and jump o'er anywhere:
  Oh 'tis my delight on a shiny night,
  In the season of the year!

1. For how long was the singer an apprentice?
2. Does this mean: (*a*) He sat idly doing nothing. (*b*) He was fastened to a piece of machinery. (*c*) He was learning a job?
3. Which two words in the first verse show that the singer was a very willing worker?
4. Does the word **poaching** in the song mean (*a*) preparing a meal of eggs in a certain way; (*b*) taking rabbits etc. from someone else's land; (*c*) repairing the front entrances of homes and cottages?
5. What were the men doing when the gamekeeper appeared?
6. What are the two lines at the end of each verse?
7. What three things were the poachers able to do very well?
8. Write out these words in full: I've; 'tis; 'twas; o'er.
9. What does the word **shiny** mean in the phrase **on a shiny night?**
10. From this list, choose words and phrases that describe the poachers' feelings when they saw the gamekeeper: terrified, nervous, bold, fearless, undaunted, unheeding, anxious, frightened, dismayed, confident, unflinching, high-spirited, bold as brass, alarmed, panic-stricken.

11. 'For him we **did not care**'. Does this mean: (*a*) They did not like him very much. (*b*) They did not see him coming. (*c*) They saw him coming, but did not worry much about him?

II. Write down the answers to the following questions:

1. What would you expect to find in a caddy: golf-clubs, people travelling, or tea?
2. Who would be likely to use a palette?
3. What do we call a place where a number of beehives are kept?
4. If you heard a cry of "Fifteen—love!", what game would be in progress?
5. What is the occupation of a joiner?
6. What do we call a person who designs a building?

III. Here are some **everyday expressions.** Choose the **phrase** that means nearly the same as the everyday expression. Example: 'To ride the high horse' means 'to be proud and snobbish'.

1. 'To **play with fire**' means (*a*) to be playing with hot coals in the grate; (*b*) to be acting a part in a pantomime; (*c*) to be taking a risk that may lead to trouble.
2. 'To **face the music**' means (*a*) to conduct the orchestra; (*b*) to be ready to face the worst that can happen; (*c*) to play music on an instrument.
3. 'To **rain cats and dogs**' means (*a*) a miraculous shower of animals; (*b*) to lead cats and dogs about on strings; (*c*) to rain very heavily indeed.

IV. Fill the spaces in the following paragraph with the required **sound-words.**

In the jungle the explorers heard the —— of the monkey and the —— of the serpents. In the distance an elephant —— and a hyena ——. They crept through the —— leaves, to the bank of a —— stream, while the temple bells —— loudly.

V. Complete these **proverbs,** or well-known sayings:

1. One good turn —— ——.
2. The early bird —— —— ——.
3. When the cat's away —— —— —— ——.
4. Every cloud has —— —— ——.

TEST 6

I. Read very carefully through the following passage, and then answer the questions.

The Presents

Jo was the first to wake in the grey dawn of Christmas morning. No stockings hung at the fireplace, and for a moment she felt disappointed. Then she remembered her mother's promise and, slipping her hand under her pillow, drew out a little crimson-covered book. She woke Meg with a "Merry Christmas", and bade her see what was under her pillow. A green-covered book appeared, with a few words written by her mother, which made the one present very precious in their eyes. Presently Beth and Amy woke, to rummage and find their little books also—one dove-coloured, the other blue; and all sat looking at, and talking about them, while the East grew rosy with the coming day.

Meg opened her new book and began to read. Jo put her arm around her, and read also, with a quiet expression on her face.

Louisa M. Alcott

1. At what season of the year did the event take place?
2. Why did Jo feel disappointed for a moment?
3. What promise had her mother made her?
4. What colour was Jo's book?
5. Who had the green book?
6. We read that the presents are **little.** Give another reason for our knowing that they are very small.
7. What made Meg's book very precious to her?
8. Write down the words actually used by Jo.
9. Jo had **a quiet expression on her face.** Which of the following words describe her: serious, excited, giggling, thoughtful, grave, amused, jaunty, pensive?
10. Write out the phrase which tells us that the sun was rising.
11. Which of these statements are correct: (*a*) Each had a solitary present. (*b*) They cared little for the presents. (*c*) They each had numerous presents. (*d*) The presents were most highly thought of?

12. What words or phrases in the story mean (*a*) to search; (*b*) told her to look; (*c*) of great value?

II. **Choosing words that are suitable**

1. Here are six **adjectives:** faithful, scientific, mountainous, shallow, famous, mischievous. Choose the most suitable to go with each of these **nouns:** mere, experiment, companion, region, elf, victory.
2. Here are six **nouns:** painting, attack, oasis, performance, taste, examination. Choose the most suitable to go with each of these **adjectives:** bitter, careful, fertile, noisy, savage, imaginative.

III. Some words have a similar sound but are spelt differently. Example: **beach, beech.** In these sentences, choose the correct word, from those in the bracket:

1. The new king ascended the **(throne, thrown).**
2. The belt was too tight for his **(waste, waist).**
3. The new **(principle, principal)** of the college was very stern.
4. John the Baptist, the **(prophet, profit),** walked through the desert.

IV. **Boy** and **toy** are rhyming words. Write these twelve words in pairs, so that they rhyme:

queue	Delhi	cow	barque	merry	new
bury	blow	jelly	though	bough	lark

V. Look at this word—**clean.** Now look at the three words inside the bracket—**(noisy, dirty, neat).** The word nearest in meaning to **clean** is **neat,** so we choose that.

Now do the same with these, choosing one word from inside the bracket each time:

1. **skill** (clumsiness, awkwardness, cleverness)
2. **curious** (unusual, ordinary, everyday)
3. **active** (sluggish, nimble, lazy)
4. **cheerful** (miserable, blithe, disappointed)
5. **wise** (witless, foolish, intelligent)
6. **belief** (trust, doubt, misgiving)

TEST 7

I. Read very carefully through the following passage, and then answer the questions.

Noah and the Dove

It came to pass at the end of forty days that Noah opened the window of the ark he had made.

And he sent forth a dove to see if the waters were abated from off the face of the earth.

But the dove found no rest for the sole of her foot, and she returned unto him, for the waters were on the face of the whole earth; then he put forth his hand and took her, and pulled her into the ark.

And he stayed yet other seven days; and again he sent forth the dove. And the dove came in to him in the evening; and lo, in her mouth was an olive leaf; so Noah knew that the waters were abated from off the earth.

And he stayed yet other seven days, and sent forth the dove which returned not again unto him.

1. How long did Noah wait before he first sent the dove?
2. What did he wish to find out?
3. Did the dove return the first time because (*a*) she wished to live in the ark; (*b*) there was nowhere she could rest; (*c*) she was frightened by hunters?
4. How long did Noah wait the second time?
5. What did the dove bring back?
6. What did this tell Noah had happened?
7. How long did Noah wait the third time?
8. Why did the dove never again return to the ark?
9. What did this tell Noah?
10. From which part of the ark did Noah release the dove?
11. What words or phrases in the story mean the same as (*a*) gone down; (*b*) behold; (*c*) it happened; (*d*) reached out?
12. Which of these would make a suitable title for the passage: (*a*) Sailing Down the Nile. (*b*) After the Deluge. (*c*) Shipwreck?

13. Here are five words: disappointing, encouraging, unrewarding, successful, fruitless. From Noah's point of view, which of them describe the dove's first flight?

II. Think about the word WALL. A **wall** need not be of **brick,** it need not be **high,** but to be a wall it must be **upright.**

Choose one word from those in the brackets that **always** has to do with the word before the bracket:

1. **quadruped**	(furry, savage, four-legged)
2. **chain**	(iron, linked, gold)
3. **plant**	(flowering, rooted, fruiting)
4. **beverage**	(hot, sweet, liquid)
5. **mountains**	(snow-capped, high, tree-clad)

III. The words in each of the following are in wrong order. Rearrange them to make sentences. (There may be more than one answer.)

1. Lost the playground in the boy book the.
2. Will be well Spring when the comes all.
3. Kindly to her speak we shall comes she when.
4. Peal lightning thunder flash of followed the of the by was.

IV. Complete these words beginning with TAR:

1. Waterproof covering.	TAR------
2. To wait for a while.	TAR--
3. We shoot arrows at it.	TAR---
4. A Scottish pattern.	TAR---
5. A deadly spider.	TAR------

V. Rewrite these sentences in the **plural** form. Example: The **girl** laid the **table.** The **girls** laid the **tables.**

1. The ship sailed safely over the reef.
2. He told me the story.
3. The boy kept the bird in the cage.
4. There was the baby in the cradle.
5. The city was destroyed by the aeroplane.
6. The boy did not play the piano well.

TEST 8

I. Read very carefully through the following passage, and then answer the questions.

A Fishing Trip

One evening during our holiday we went on a fishing trip. A car called for us after dinner and took us to Duntulm. There, three boats were waiting in the cove. Gradually the party was sorted out, and we went aboard.

We sat in a semi-circle in the stern of our boat, holding long bamboo poles in our hands. The lines trailed behind the boat which was propelled by two crofters, turned fishermen for the evening. We did not use bait. Instead, each hook had on it a twist of frayed twine. As it moved through the water, the stupid fish rushed and fought with one another to swallow it and be caught. As fast as we took one fish off the hook, another was waiting there in the deep, dark water to take its place. The bottom of the boat was soon covered.

1. At what time of day did the fishing trip begin?
2. How did the fishers reach the starting place?
3. How many boats were there?
4. **The party was sorted out.** Does this mean (*a*) the passage money was collected; (*b*) the people were divided into groups; (*c*) the picnic-hampers were unpacked, and the feast began?
5. What was used instead of bait?
6. Why was it unnecessary to use real bait?
7. Why were the fish said to be stupid?
8. What words are used to describe the water in the cove?
9. What is meant by **crofters turned fishermen for the evening?**
10. What words or phrases in the story mean (*a*) half-circle; (*b*) foolish; (*c*) little by little; (*d*) went into the boats; (*e*) rowed by?
11. Write down the **opposites** of these words taken from the story: stupid, aboard, evening, stern, behind, covered.

II. The word **bark** has more than one meaning. It means 'the outside of a tree', and 'the sound made by a dog'. Write down the words that fit in with the following descriptions:

1. A colour; an animal.
2. A burial place; serious.
3. A plant; where coins are made.
4. To stagger; a lively dance; on which cotton is wound.
5. A tree; to make wood smooth.

III. Look at this:

(pretty, beautiful, lovely)—(ugly, **charming,** untidy)

Of the three words in the second bracket, the word **charming** is nearest in meaning to the three words in the first bracket.

Now do the same with these:

1. (excitable, fussy, fidgety)—(impatient, tranquil, calm)
2. (skill, cleverness, ability)—(clumsiness, talent, dullness)
3. (pursuing, chasing, seeking)—(avoiding, hunting, evading)
4. (king, emperor, sovereign)—(vassal, retainer, monarch)
5. (freedom, independence, liberty)—(bondage, self-government, serfdom)
6. (knowledge, insight, learning)—(ignorance, comprehension, confusion)

IV. We speak of **a** boy, **a** house, but **an** egg and **an** apple.

Write **a** or **an** in the space in the following sentences:

1. He travelled through —— African jungle in search of —— orchid.
2. Mary took —— hour and —— half to do the job.
3. Which do you prefer, —— excellent report or —— prize?
4. Pick me —— orange, but not —— unripe one.

V. **Jumbled Words.** Find the names of these animals.

Example: TOGA becomes GOAT.

1. ZEGELLA	2. ARJGAU	3. ANYEH
4. AMALL	5. ALIGORL	6. SBNIO

TEST 9

I. Read very carefully through the following passage, and then answer the questions.

The Floating Mine

The mine was within a stone's throw of the wall. It seemed certain that nothing could prevent an explosion that would wreck the work of the treasure-seekers, undo the toil of months, and write the word 'Finish' to the whole scheme.

"It's now or never," muttered Jim. He poised himself on the edge of the wall, bare toes gripping the concrete like a competitor in a swimming-race waiting for the starter's whistle.

Jim's swallow-dive was perfect. He broke surface and swam deliberately towards the black menace that was drifting with the current in his direction. He reached the mine and was treading water alongside it, looking vainly for some projection which he might grasp. The only projections were the deadly horns themselves. "Here goes," he said. He turned over on his back and waited until the mine was touching him.

1. What operation was going on in the story?
2. What was the danger that threatened?
3. Of what material was the top of the wall made?
4. Jim's dive was called a **swallow-dive** because (*a*) he swallowed a lot of sea-water; (*b*) he dived off a wall; (*c*) he cut through the air like a swallow. Which of these?
5. He swam **deliberately.** Does this mean: (*a*) He approached the mine in a roundabout way. (*b*) He swam towards it, straight and calmly. (*c*) He swam underwater?
6. Why was the mine called **a black menace?**
7. The mine was **a stone's throw** away. Was this distance about (*a*) five hundred feet; (*b*) five feet; (*c*) fifty feet?
8. Write the words actually spoken by Jim.
9. What words or phrases in the story mean (*a*) without success; (*b*) came to the surface; (*c*) the parts sticking out; (*d*) swimming on the same spot?

10. Write down the title or titles that are suitable for this story:
    (*a*) Routine Work for Jim. (*b*) A Hazardous Undertaking.
    (*c*) A Solo Effort.

II. Rewrite this paragraph using a **capital letter** at the beginning of each **proper noun:**

jones and smith took part in a stand of two hundred runs for the school against peatborough. The visiting captain, drake, tried seven bowlers, of whom jorkins was the most successful. The river severn flowed past the ground on its way to the bristol channel, and all loamshire was peaceful on this fine june day. It was a field-day for the pupils of meadowcroft grammar school. jones was their hero.

III. Write these **in order of size,** beginning with the smallest:

1. dromedary, rabbit, tiger, elephant, mouse
2. melon, cherry, grapefruit, plum, lemon
3. wind, breeze, gale, hurricane, zephyr
4. cod, shark, minnow, herring, sprat

IV. From the words inside the bracket in each sentence, write down the one word that is nearest in meaning to the word in front of the sentence.

Example: **annually.** The book was published (daily, weekly, **yearly**).

1. **opponent** John's (confederate, antagonist, colleague) soon arrived.
2. **climb** It is time for us to (envisage, ascend, descend) the mountain.
3. **soothing** The drink from the bottle proved most (tranquillizing, worrying, disturbing).
4. **courage** You have shown great (bravery, fear, cowardice).

V. Pears, plums, apples, cherries are all **fruits.** Write down one word for each of these groups:

1. slowly, quickly, stealthily, hurriedly, easily
2. emerald, amethyst, topaz, ruby, turquoise
3. crab, lobster, shrimp, prawn, crayfish
4. Christianity, Buddhism, Islam, Hinduism, Judaism

TEST 10

I. Read very carefully through the following verses, and then answer the questions.

The Wind in a Frolic

But the wind had swept on, and had met in a lane
With a schoolboy, who panted and struggled in vain;
For it tossed him and twirled him, then passed—and he stood
With his hat in a pool, and his shoes in the mud!

Then away went the wind in its holiday glee,
And now it was far on the billowy sea:
And the lordly ships felt its staggering blow,
And the little boats darted to and fro.

But lo! it was night, and it sank to rest
On the sea-birds' rock in the gleaming west,
Laughing to think, in its frolicsome fun,
How little of mischief it really had done.

William Howitt

1. How do we know that the wind had been somewhere else before it met the schoolboy?
2. From this list, choose words and phrases that describe the boy after the wind had gone by: clean, spotless, begrimed, spruce, bespattered, unsoiled, bedaubed, immaculate, untidy, dishevelled, clean as a new pin, in disorder, tidy, confused.
3. What did the wind do (*a*) to the big ships; (*b*) to the small boats?
4. Where did the wind finally settle down to rest?
5. The sea was **billowy.** Explain the word in heavy type.
6. Explain the difference between (*a*) the sea-birds' rock, and (*b*) the sea-bird's rock.
7. From these words and phrases choose those that might describe the wind's behaviour: playful, jocular, melancholy, grave, light-hearted, playful as a kitten, down in the dumps, frolicsome.

II. Choose, from the word in brackets, the most suitable word to finish the line of poetry:

1. In winter, when the fields are white,
   I sing this song for your **(pleasure, delight, happiness).**
   In spring, when woods are getting green,
   I'll try and tell you what I **(think, wish, mean).**
2. A man of words and not of deeds,
   Is like a garden full of **(plants, weeds, docks);**
   And when the weeds begin to grow,
   It's like a garden full of **(rain, ice, snow).**

III. Look at this:

Country—France; **People**—French; **Language**—French.
Now complete these lists:

Country	People	Language
1. Denmark	?	?
2. Spain	?	?
3. Norway	?	?
4. Greenland	?	?

IV. Beginning with the word CLOAK, and changing only one letter at a time, we can make the word BLACK, in this way: CLOAK, CLOCK, BLOCK, BLACK. We call this a **word ladder.**

Now do these:

1.	CLOWN	2.	RIVER
Worn by a king	- - - - -	One who roams	- - - - -
Sing quietly	- - - - -	He propels a boat	- - - - -
Shepherd's staff	- - - - -		SOWER
	BROOK		

V. Write down this passage as it should be written, in verse. Begin each line with a **capital letter:**

At the corner of Wood Street, when daylight appears, hangs a thrush that sings loud, it has sung for three years. Poor Susan has passed by the spot and has heard, in the silence of the morning, the song of that bird.

TEST 11

I. Read very carefully through the following passage, and then answer the questions.

The Chibchas

There once was a race of people who lived in Colombia. They were the Chibchas, and they were somewhat similar to the Aztecs of Mexico. They believed that at the bottom of a certain lake lived a god called the Gilded Man, who could be kept good-tempered only by offerings of the most valuable kind. These offerings had to be numerous and frequent. So, at every full moon, when the lake itself shone like a great sheet of gold, the priests would load their canoes with offerings and, at a certain spot in the lake, the god's dwelling-place, would cast them overboard, after repeating many prayers.

Now, as gold was very common to the Chibchas, and as the Gilded Man was accustomed only to the very best, they made beautiful ornaments and decorated them with precious stones, before casting them overboard.

1. Where did the Chibchas live?
2. Where did the Aztecs live?
3. What was the name of the Chibcha god?
4. Where was this god thought to be living?
5. What was the Chibcha way of trying to please their god?
6. When did the Chibchas make their offerings?
7. What did they do before making their offerings?
8. Why was it a simple matter for the Chibchas to make offerings of gold?
9. How did they make their offerings even more valuable?
10. What words or phrases in the story mean (*a*) costly; (*b*) much the same as; (*c*) throw; (*d*) plentiful and often; (*e*) used to having?
11. If this story were described as **mythical** or **legendary**, what would that mean?

12. Give two meanings of the word **race.**
13. Write down a phrase opposite in meaning to **numerous and frequent.**

II. Look at this:

Country—France; **Money**— ? **Answer:** francs

Now complete these lists:

	Country	**Money**		**Country**	**Money**
1.	U.S.S.R.	?	4.	?	marks
2.	U.S.A.	?	5.	?	lire
3.	Switzerland	?	6.	?	rupees

III. Name the characters from fiction described below.

1. A one-legged sailor with a parrot.
2. He made seven voyages to exciting places.
3. A young man who came out of the west.
4. Everything he touched turned to gold.
5. He stole Helen away and took her to Troy.
6. They sailed away in a sieve.

IV. A **splinter** is a very small piece **of wood.** Here are some other small amounts:

grain ray breath pinch morsel drop

Choose the correct ones to use with these words:

snuff water food air light sand

V. Rewrite the sentences below, filling each space with the correct word from this list: **who, whose, whom, what.** (You may use some words more than once.)

1. This is the boy —— coat was stolen.
2. I should like to know —— threw the stone.
3. Do you know to —— you are speaking?
4. Can you see —— I see?
5. —— do you wish to meet?
6. —— ball is that?

TEST 12

I. Read very carefully through the following passage, and then answer the questions.

Tom's First Sight Of Rugby School

" Here's Rugby, sir, at last. You'll be in plenty of time for dinner," said the old guard, pulling his horn out of its case, and tootle-tooing away on it.

The coachman shook up his horses and carried them along the side of the school close. Tom's heart beat quickly as he passed the great field, in which several games of football were going on. He tried to take in at once the great, long line of grey buildings, beginning with the chapel, and ending with the school-house, the residence of the headmaster, where the great flag was lazily waving from the highest round tower. He began already to be proud of being a Rugby boy, as he passed through the school gates and saw the boys standing there, looking as if the town belonged to them, and nodding in a familiar way to the coachman.

Thomas Hughes

1. How had Tom travelled to Rugby?
2. Tom **tried to take in at once.** What does this phrase mean?
3. On which building was the flagstaff?
4. How do we know that the field was very large?
5. Which building was first, and which was last in line?
6. How do we know that it was **not** the summer term that was beginning?
7. Write down the adjectives used to describe (*a*) the buildings; (*b*) the guard; (*c*) the field; (*d*) the tower.
8. How can we tell that the boys knew the coachman quite well?
9. Why did the guard carry the horn: (*a*) to strike people who tried to jump on to the coach without permission; (*b*) to carry refreshment for the journey; (*c*) to give warning of the approach of the coach?
10. What are the words **tootle-tooing** supposed to represent?
11. Name the two persons in charge of the coach.
12. How do we know that the journey had been a long one?

13. From this list, choose words that might describe Tom's feelings at the time: proud, happy, bored, dismayed, interested, attentive, terrified, delighted, sorrowful, observant, enthusiastic, absorbed.
14. What words or phrases in the story mean (*a*) the headmaster's house; (*b*) Tom became excited; (*c*) roused the horses: (*d*) drove along the side of; (*e*) the grounds belonging to the school?

II. Complete the words below using either ERY or ARY:

1. The train was standing still. It was	STATION---
2. He rode across the desert on a	DROMED---
3. Remember to oil the	MACHIN---
4. The shop sold tobacco and	CONFECTION---
5. I am suspicious. There has been some	ROGU---

III. Change these sentences, which are in the Present Tense, to the Past Tense:

1. I forget my address.
2. I write a letter.
3. He knows his part.
4. They kneel in prayer.
5. We shake hands.
6. He chooses the red one.

IV. Write out these sentences, putting the **apostrophe** in its correct place:

Example: It was Toms cap. It was Tom's cap.

1. The book fell off the teachers desk.
2. The boy knocked at the door of the teachers (several) room.
3. A mans hat blew off.
4. The mens club was closed for decoration.
5. The babies bottles were washed.
6. The babys mother was taken ill.

V. Change these sentences from **indirect speech** to **direct speech.**

Example: The boy said that he broke the window. The boy said: "I broke the window."

1. The teacher asked who came late for prayers.
2. The umpire said that the batsman was out.
3. The judge wrote that he thought the prisoner was guilty.
4. The announcer said that heavy falls of snow were expected.

TEST 13

I. Read very carefully through the following passage, and then answer the questions.

The Hunt

Pwyll, Prince of Dyfed, was minded to go and hunt. So he set forth from Narberth that night and, early on the morrow, he came to a wood. He let loose the dogs, sounded the horn, and began the chase. Whilst he listened to the hounds, he heard the cry of other hounds, a cry different from his own, coming in the opposite direction.

He beheld a glade in the wood, forming a level plain, and as his dogs came to the edge of the glade, he saw a stag before the other dogs. And lo! as it reached the middle of the glade, the dogs that followed the stag overtook it and brought it down. And as he came towards the dogs and drove those away that had brought down the stag, he saw a horseman coming towards him upon a light grey steed.

Lady Charlotte Guest

1. Put into your own words **was minded to go and hunt.**
2. The pack of hounds which he took were probably (*a*) fox hounds; (*b*) otter hounds; (*c*) stag hounds; (*d*) wolf hounds. Which of these?
3. Did Pwyll ride through the morning, the afternoon, the evening, or the night?
4. Put these into the order in which they happened: (*a*) He sounded the horn. (*b*) He heard another pack of hounds. (*c*) He let loose his own dogs. (*d*) He came to a wood.
5. How did Pwyll know that there was another pack of hounds in the wood even before he had seen them?
6. Which pack reached the animal first, Pwyll's or the stranger's?
7. Who rode the light grey steed, Pwyll or the stranger?
8. What words or phrases in the story mean (*a*) an open space in the wood; (*b*) saw; (*c*) horse?
9. Write down any three words or phrases no longer in everyday use that tell us this story was written some time ago.

10. In this sentence, explain the two words in heavy type: 'The hounds began to **bay** as the stag was brought to **bay**'.
11. From these, choose the most suitable title for the story: (*a*) Many Follow the Hounds. (*b*) A Strange Meeting in the Wood. (*c*) No Sign of the Stag.

II. When we hear the word **doctor** we may think of the word **patient.**

Write down the words that we usually pair with those printed below:

1. Guest and ——	4. Parent and ——
2. Leader and ——	5. Town and ——
3. Teacher and ——	6. Hill and ——

III. Each of the following words begins with **ph,** that sounds as **f.**

1. Taken with a camera.
2. Highly inflammable chemical used in the manufacture of matches.
3. Doctor.
4. A large town in the U.S.A.
5. A person who collects stamps.
6. A game-bird.

IV. A lion's home is a **den.** In what do these animals live?

1. badger	2. beaver	3. squirrel
4. eagle	5. fox	6. otter

V. Rewrite the paragraph below, using a word from the list given to fill each of the spaces:

breath	forget	almost	feeding	smoke
railway	palings	strange	before	clatter

I shall never —— the first train that I saw. I was —— quietly near the —— that separated the meadow from the ——, when I heard a —— sound at a distance, and —— I knew whence it came, with a rush, ——, and a puffing out of ——, a long, black train of something flew by and was gone —— before I could draw ——.

TEST 14

I. Read very carefully through the following passage, and then answer the questions.

The Sleeping Warriors

In an enormous cavern somewhere in Scotland lie hundreds of sleeping warriors. They have slumbered for centuries. Their horses are asleep, too. They await the breaking of a spell placed upon them hundreds of years ago. They sleep until the time comes when Scotland shall need them.

Outside the cavern hangs a horn upon which three blasts must be blown to rouse the sleepers to action. Once only has the horn been sounded, when a great crisis arose, and the men were needed. Someone went to rouse them. He blew the first blast. The warriors awoke and raised themselves upon their elbows. The horses shook their harness, and champed their bits. This so terrified the messenger that he fled.

There they lie in the darkness of the cavern, awaiting the second and the third blasts that will never come. The horn is still there, too. But alas! no one knows where the cavern is.

1. Why are the men and horses asleep in the cavern?
2. When, according to the story, will they awaken?
3. How many times must the horn now be blown?
4. What is another word for **hundreds of years?**
5. When the horn blew, what happened (*a*) to the men; (*b*) to the horses?
6. What effect did this have upon the blower?
7. Why has no one gone to rouse the sleepers since that time?
8. It was necessary to arouse the sleepers because **a great crisis arose.** What do these words mean?
9. The horses **champed their bits.** Does this mean (*a*) they moved their mouthpieces with their teeth and made a rattling sound; (*b*) they tried to find a champion amongst themselves; (*c*) they ate their food?

10. From this list, choose words and phrases that describe the man after he had blown the horn: frightened, alarmed, undismayed, panic-stricken, unafraid, brave as a lion, bold as brass, white as a sheet, with hair on end, valiant, terror-stricken, unflinching, composed.

II. A **young lion** is a **cub.** Write down the names for the young of the following animals:

1. elephant	2. gander	3. stag
4. swan	5. hare	6. frog

III. Paul's work is **good,** Peter's work is **better,** but Philip's work is the **best** of the three.

In the same way, fill in the spaces in the following sentences:

1. Jim could run **fast,** Jane could run ——, but Joe could run the ——.
2. John is **ignorant,** David is —— ——, but Bill is the —— ——.
3. Mary had **many** sums right, Jane had ——, but Susan had ——.
4. Cherries are **juicy,** plums are ——, but oranges are —— of all.

IV. From the adjective **brave** we can make the noun **bravery.**

Make a noun from the adjective in front of each of the following sentences, and use it to fill the space.

1. **anxious**	He showed some —— over the result of the test.
2. **beautiful**	The film-star was renowned for her great ——.
3. **abundant**	There was an —— of food on the table.
4. **prosperous**	There was —— throughout the land.
5. **faithful**	You must have —— in what I am doing.

V. Fill the spaces in the following paragraph with suitable **sound-words:**

There were bird sounds everywhere. The parrot was ——, the owl was ——, and the eagle was ——. Added to this, a hound —— outside, and a mouse —— in the wainscot. Mark —— the coins in his pocket; then with a —— of hoofs, and a —— of brakes, the coach came to a standstill.

TEST 15

I. Read very carefully through the following verses, and then answer the questions.

What I See

Behold! a giant am I!
  Aloft here in my tower
  With my granite jaws I devour
The maize, the wheat, and the rye,
  And grind them into flour.

I look down over the farms;
  In the fields of grain I see
  The harvest that is to be,
And I fling aloft my arms,
  For I know it is all for me.

I hear the sound of flails
  Far off from the threshing floors,
  In barns with their open doors,
And the wind, the wind in my sails
  Louder and louder roars.

H. W. Longfellow

1. Who or what is speaking: (*a*) an ogre; (*b*) a windmill; (*c*) a farmer of giant size?
2. What were the **granite jaws?**
3. Give one word for maize, wheat, and rye.
4. The word **devour** means (*a*) admire; (*b*) ignore; (*c*) consume. Which of these?
5. Why were the jaws made of granite, and not of sandstone, or chalk?
6. Why was the **giant** able to look over the farms and fields?
7. What were the **arms** that he was flinging to the air?
8. Was he happy at what he saw because (*a*) he liked destroying things; (*b*) the things he wanted always fought against him; (*c*) he knew that there would be plenty of work for him to do?

ANSWERS

Test 1

I. 1. The magic bulls leaped out.
2. There were two bulls.
3. They breathed out flames.
4. They rushed upon him with lowered heads.
5. He flinched never a step.
6. He wrestled with the nearest bull.
7. He made them plough the sacred land.
8. He used a lance.
9. He sowed the serpents' teeth.
10. (*a*) singed; (*b*) goaded; (*c*) sacred; (*d*) waited what would befall
11. extraordinary, magical, remarkable, notable, eventful, impressive, fantastic
12. (*b*) Taken from a Greek Myth

II. 1. (*c*) a lion 2. (*b*) a fox 3. (*a*) a mule
4. (*b*) a mountain-goat 5. (*c*) a berry 6. (*b*) a mouse

III. hedge-sparrow, collar-bone, sea-chest, flower-bed, tooth-brush, quarter-deck

IV. 1. spectators 2. audience 3. congregation 4. mob

V. 1. We saw the banjos on the tables.
2. The babies opened the boxes.
3. Our brothers-in-law served as fighter-pilots.
4. The girls chased the thieves.
5. The hunters fired on the wolves.
6. The salmon and the trout swam safely away.

Test 2

I. 1. They had been searching for the chart.
2. It had come from the marshes around the camp.
3. They had been painted white with gilt decorations.
4. They bore marks made by the pirates' dirty hands.
5. They had been used as spills for lighting pipes.
6. The lamp was still burning.
7. Wines and spirits in casks and bottles were stored there.
8. The rolling of the ship made the bottles clink.

9. (*a*) lockfast places; (*b*) ruffians; (*c*) in quest of; (*d*) consult; (*e*) gutted out
10. slimy, unkempt, foul, offensive, confused, beastly, unattractive
11. mutineers
12. (*b*) Inconsiderate Visitors to a Vessel
13. drunk, clean, closed (shut), ended (finished)

II. 1. He and I are going to the football match.
2. Who is the cleverer now, Tom or Harry?
3. It is a pity that the footballer has broken his leg. (**or** broke)
4. Give him those books to read.

III. 1. flotsam 2. survivors 3. lagoon
4. summit (top) 5. panorama 6. decided (determined)

IV. 1. stationary 2. opaque 3. contracts 4. minimum

V. Adams, Andrews, Atkins, Brown, Browning, Bruce, Chivers, Clark, Clarke, Davies, Davis, Duncan

Test 3

I. 1. She could not dine without him.
2. It was on the queen's table, close to her left elbow.
3. He had a set of silver dishes and plates.
4. They were kept in a silver box in the nurse's pocket.
5. It was the nurse's duty.
6. Gulliver, the queen, her two daughters and Glumdalclitch
7. One was sixteen years old; the other was thirteen years and one month.
8. They are called the two princesses royal.
9. (*a*) entire; (*b*) necessaries; (*c*) in proportion to; (*d*) save
10. **Queen:** gigantic, enormous, tremendous, large, Brobdingnagian, lusty, vast, towering, mountainous, lofty
Gulliver: dwarfish, tiny, diminutive, pygmy, little
11. (*a*) cannot be proved; (*b*) true; (*c*) true; (*d*) untrue; (*e*) cannot be proved; (*f*) untrue

II. 1. British Broadcasting Corporation; Independent Television Authority; Very High Frequency
2. British Airways; Transworld Airline
3. Detective Inspector; Criminal Investigation Department
4. Able-bodied seaman; Her Majesty's Ship; Victoria Cross

III. 1. key 2. tongs 3. go 4. square

IV. Sentences 3, 4, 2, 5, 1.

V.
1. She gave her the vixen for a present.
2. The huntress chased the hind.
3. The shepherdess rode after her flock on a mare.
4. My mother-in-law is a countess.

Test 4

I.
1. The trees leaned forward.
2. crept closer and closer; shake tops with their neighbours
3. They were the chug-chug of the launch and the conversations of the natives.
4. It was monotonous because the noise continued without changing.
5. They saw the falls when the launch swung round the bend.
6. The falling water of the cascade caused the booming sound.
7. The sun shining on the spray showed the colours of the rainbow.
8. The water falling from a great height caused the spray.
9. (*a*) impenetrable; (*b*) cascade; (*c*) neighbours; (*d*) vegetation
10. (*a*) fascinated; (*b*) hypnotised; (*c*) astonished; (*d*) amazed; (*e*) astounded; (*f*) stupefied; (*g*) petrified; (*h*) dumbfounded
11. (*b*) After a time, the river became much narrower. (*d*) A most beautiful sight met their eyes.

II.
1. The rocket, red in colour, soared into the air.
2. "There is a ship on the reef!" exclaimed Paul.
3. "Is she in great danger?" the stranger asked.
4. "She'll hold, but don't be too long," was the reply.

III. 1. beautiful 2. pansy 3. nowhere 4. waiting 5. hasty 6. wise

IV. 1. Saturday 2. untrue 3. puck 4. chrysalis 5. Eskimo

V. 1. CEILING 2. FIELD 3. PENCIL 4. CEREAL 5. CURRANT 6. GRATEFUL

Test 5

I.
1. He was an apprentice for more than seven years.
2. (*c*) He was learning a job.
3. Full well
4. (*b*) taking rabbits etc. from someone else's land

5. They were setting a snare.
6. These lines are the chorus (refrain).
7. They were able to wrestle, fight and jump.
8. I have it is; it was; over
9. It means 'when the moon is shining brightly'.
10. bold, fearless, undaunted, unheeding, confident, unflinching, high-spirited, bold as brass
11. (*c*) They saw him coming, but did not worry much about him.

II. 1. tea 2. an artist 3. an apiary 4. lawn tennis
5. making wooden furniture, fittings, etc. 6. an architect

III. 1. (*c*) to be taking a risk that may lead to trouble
2. (*b*) to be ready to face the worst that can happen
3. (*c*) to rain very heavily indeed

IV. chattering, hissing, trumpeted, screamed, rustling, murmuring (babbling, gurgling), pealed

V. 1. deserves another 2. catches the worm
3. the mice will play 4. silver lining

Test 6

I. 1. It took place at Christmas-time.
2. She was disappointed because no stockings were hanging at the fireplace.
3. She had promised to place a small gift for each under their pillows.
4. It was crimson.
5. Meg had the green book.
6. They were placed under the girls' pillows.
7. Her mother had written something in it.
8. "Merry Christmas"
9. serious, thoughtful, grave, pensive
10. The East grew rosy with the coming day.
11. (*a*) Each had a solitary present. (*d*) The presents were most highly thought of.
12. (*a*) rummage; (*b*) bade her see; (*c*) very precious

II. 1. faithful companion; scientific experiment; mountainous region; shallow mere; famous victory; mischievous elf
2. imaginative painting; savage attack; fertile oasis; noisy performance; bitter taste; careful examination

III. 1. throne 2. waist 3. principal 4. prophet

IV. queue, new; Delhi, jelly; barque, lark; cow, bough; merry, bury; blow, though

V. 1. cleverness 2. unusual 3. nimble. 4. blithe 5. intelligent 6. trust

Test 7

I.
1. He waited for forty days.
2. He wished to find out if the floods had gone down.
3. (*b*) there was nowhere she could rest
4. He waited for seven days.
5. She brought back an olive leaf.
6. It told him that the floods had gone down, because trees had appeared and were sprouting.
7. He waited another seven days.
8. She did not return because she found trees to perch in and food to eat.
9. The floods had now gone down completely and dry land had appeared.
10. He released her from a window.
11. (*a*) abated; (*b*) lo; (*c*) it came to pass; (*d*) put forth his hand
12. (*b*) After the Deluge
13. disappointing, unrewarding, fruitless

II. 1. four-legged 2. linked 3. rooted 4. liquid 5. high

III.
1. The boy lost the book in the playground.
2. When the Spring comes all will be well.
3. We shall speak kindly to her when she comes.
4. The flash of lightning was followed by a peal of thunder.

IV. 1. TARPAULIN 2. TARRY 3. TARGET 4. TARTAN 5. TARANTULA

V.
1. The ships sailed safely over the reefs.
2. They told us the stories.
3. The boys kept the birds in the cages.
4. There were the babies in the cradles.
5. The cities were destroyed by the aeroplanes.
6. The boys did not play the pianos well.

Test 8

I. 1. It began in the evening, after dinner.
2. They went there by car.
3. There were three boats.
4. (*b*) the people were divided into groups
5. A twist of frayed twine was used instead.
6. The fish were easily attracted by the frayed string.
7. They rushed at the hook and fought to catch it.
8. The water was deep and dark.
9. They were really crofters (farmers), but for that evening they were helping with the fishing.
10. (*a*) semi-circle; (*b*) stupid; (*c*) gradually; (*d*) went aboard; (*e*) propelled by
11. wise, ashore, morning, bows, before, uncovered

II. 1. fawn 2. grave 3. mint 4. reel 5. plane

III. 1. impatient 2. talent 3. hunting 4. monarch 5. self-government 6. comprehension

IV. 1. an, an 2. an, a 3. an, a 4. an, an

V. 1. GAZELLE 2. JAGUAR 3. HYENA 4. LLAMA 5. GORILLA 6. BISON

Test 9

I. 1. A hunt for treasure was in progress.
2. It was feared that a floating mine would explode.
3. It was made of concrete.
4. (*c*) he cut through the air like a swallow
5. (*b*) He swam towards it, straight and calmly.
6. It was black in colour, and highly dangerous.
7. (*c*) fifty feet
8. "It's now or never," and "Here goes."
9. (*a*) vainly; (*b*) broke surface; (*c*) projections; (*d*) treading water
10. (*b*) A Hazardous Undertaking (*c*) A Solo Effort

II. Jones, Smith, Peatborough, Drake, Jorkins, River Severn, Bristol Channel, Loamshire, June, Meadowcroft Grammar School, Jones

III. 1. mouse, rabbit, tiger, dromedary, elephant
2. cherry, plum, lemon, grapefruit, melon
3. zephyr, breeze, wind, gale, hurricane
4. minnow, sprat, herring, cod, shark

IV. 1. antagonist 2. ascend 3. tranquillizing 4. bravery

V. 1. adverbs 2. precious stones 3. shellfish 4. religions

Test 10

I. 1. We are told that the wind had swept on.

2. begrimed, bespattered, bedaubed, untidy, dishevelled, in disorder, confused
3. (*a*) It dealt them staggering blows. (*b*) It blew them to and fro on the sea.
4. It settled on the sea-birds' rock in the ocean.
5. Its surface was disturbed by waves.
6. (*a*) a rock inhabited by many sea-birds; (*b*) a rock inhabited by one sea-bird
7. playful, jocular, light-hearted, playful as a kitten, frolicsome

II. 1. delight, mean 2. weeds, snow

III.

1. Denmark	Danes	Danish
2. Spain	Spaniards	Spanish
3. Norway	Norwegians	Norwegian
4. Greenland	Eskimos	Eskimo

IV. 1. CLOWN, CROWN, CROON, CROOK, BROOK

2. RIVER, ROVER, ROWER, SOWER

V. At the corner of Wood Street, when daylight appears,
Hangs a thrush that sings loud, it has sung for three years.
Poor Susan has passed by the spot and has heard,
In the silence of the morning, the song of that bird.

Test 11

I. 1. They lived in Colombia.

2. The Aztecs lived in Mexico.
3. He was called the Gilded Man.
4. He was thought to live at the bottom of a certain lake.
5. They made valuable offerings to him.
6. They made them at full moon.
7. They repeated many prayers.
8. There was plenty of gold in their country.
9. They decorated them with precious stones.
10. (*a*) valuable; (*b*) somewhat similar; (*c*) cast; (*d*) numerous and frequent; (*e*) was accustomed to
11. It would mean that the events described were imaginary, and did not really happen.

12. a tribe of people; to compete with others at running, etc.
13. few and infrequent

II. 1. roubles 4. Germany
2. dollars 5. Italy
3. francs 6. India

III. 1. Long John Silver 2. Sinbad the Sailor 3. Young Lochinvar
4. King Midas 5. Paris 6. The Jumblies

IV. grain of sand; ray of light; breath of air; pinch of snuff; morsel of food; drop of water

V. 1. whose 2. who 3. whom 4. what
5. Whom 6. Whose

Test 12

I. 1. He had travelled by stage-coach.
2. He looked quickly from one building to another.
3. It was on the school-house, the headmaster's residence.
4. Several games of football were being played at the same time.
5. The chapel was first and the school-house was last.
6. Games of football were being played.
7. (*a*) grey; (*b*) old; (*c*) great; (*d*) round
8. They nodded to him in a familiar way.
9. (*c*) to give warning of the approach of the coach
10. They represent the noise made when the horn was blown.
11. They were the guard and the coachman.
12. The guard said "at last".
13. proud, happy, interested, attentive, delighted, observant, enthusiastic, absorbed
14. (*a*) the residence of the headmaster (the school-house); (*b*) Tom's heart beat quickly; (*c*) shook up his horses; (*d*) carried them along the side of; (*e*) the school close

II. 1. STATIONARY 2. DROMEDARY 3. MACHINERY
4. CONFECTIONERY 5. ROGUERY

III. 1. I forgot my address. 4. They knelt in prayer.
2. I wrote a letter. 5. We shook hands.
3. He knew his part. 6. He chose the red one.

IV. 1. teacher's 2. teachers' 3. man's 4. men's
5. babies' 6. baby's

V. 1. The teacher asked: "Who came late for prayers?"
2. The umpire said: "The batsman is out."
3. The judge wrote: "I think the prisoner is guilty."
4. The announcer said: "Heavy falls of snow are expected."

Test 13

I. 1. made up his mind to go hunting
2. (*c*) stag hounds
3. He rode through the night.
4. (*d*), (*c*), (*a*) and (*b*)
5. He heard the cry of the other pack.
6. The stranger's pack reached it first.
7. The stranger rode the grey steed.
8. (*a*) a glade; (*b*) beheld; (*c*) steed
9. minded to go, set forth, morrow, beheld, lo! (three of these)
10. 'Began to bay' means 'began to bark'. 'Brought to bay' means 'unable to run any farther, so turns to face the hounds'.
11. (*b*) A Strange Meeting in the Wood

II. 1. host
2. follower
3. pupil
4. child
5. country
6. dale

III. 1. photograph
2. phosphorus
3. physician
4. Philadelphia
5. philatelist
6. pheasant

IV. 1. set (earth)
2. lodge
3. drey
4. eyrie
5. earth
6. holt

V. forget, feeding, palings, railway, strange, before, clatter, smoke, almost, breath

Test 14

I. 1. A spell has been placed upon them.
2. They will awaken when Scotland has need of them.
3. It must be blown twice.
4. centuries
5. (*a*) The men awoke and raised themselves upon their elbows.
(*b*) The horses shook their harness and clamped their bits.
6. He was terrified and fled.
7. No one knows where the cavern is.
8. Something unusual had happened; Scotland was in danger.

9. (*a*) they moved their mouthpieces with their teeth, and made a rattling sound
10. frightened, alarmed, panic-stricken, white as a sheet, with hair on end, terror-stricken

II. 1. calf 2. gosling 3. fawn 4. cygnet 5. leveret 6. tadpole

III. 1. faster, fastest 2. more ignorant, most ignorant 3. more, most 4. juicier, juiciest

IV. 1. anxiety 2. beauty 3. abundance 4. prosperity 5. faith

V. screeching, hooting, screaming, bayed, squeaked, jingled, clatter, grinding

Test 15

I.
1. (*b*) a windmill
2. They were the millstones.
3. grain (corn)
4. (*c*) consume
5. Granite is a hard stone which would grind the corn into flour; sandstone or chalk, being softer stones, would wear themselves out.
6. The windmill was a tall building, possibly on a hill, to catch the wind.
7. The arms were the sails.
8. (*c*) he knew that there would be plenty of work for him to do
9. enormous, gigantic, tremendous, huge
10. (*c*) A Rural Scene

II. 1. adventurous 2. sorrowful 3. southerly 4. gigantic 5. circular

III. 1. to 2. in 3. with 4. from 5. of

IV. 1. grocer 2. fishmonger 3. stationer 4. greengrocer 5. confectioner 6. ironmonger

V. 1. nephew 2. radish 3. apricot 4. evil 5. yellow

Test 16

I.
1. They slept in a cave.
2. (*a*) heather bushes; (*b*) Alan's greatcoat
3. They were in a low, hidden place in the glen.

4. It was used (*a*) to warm them; (*b*) to cook the porridge; (*c*) to grill the trout.
5. It means a brook.
6. They wished for salt.
7. appetising, palatable, undersized, inconsiderable
8. (*c*) the oats from which the porridge was made
9. (*a*) pleasure; (*b*) business
10. (*a*) glen; (*b*) when the clouds set in; (*c*) grill
11. (*b*) with the hands

II. 1. knowledge 2. education 3. grief
4. negligence (neglect) 5. imitation

III. 1. The sheep browsed alongside the houses.
2. Our sons-in-law fired the cannon.
3. They seized the glowing splinters with the tongs.
4. They stalked the deer through the mountain passes.
5. The sheath knives gradually cut through the thongs.
6. The cartons contained tasty cheeses.

IV. 1. Peter Pan 2. Smike 3. Little John
4. Oliver Twist 5. Gulliver 6. The Owl and the Pussy-cat

V.

1. Belgium	Belgians	Flemish (French)
2. Finland	Finns	Finnish
3. Turkey	Turks	Turkish
4. Mexico	Mexicans	Spanish

Test 17

I. 1. They made various kinds of clothes.
2. The clothes in which they had landed were very ragged.
3. This was to allow for the turn-up to overlap the foot.
4. It was easier to make holes in wet leather.
5. They were to take strings or laces that could be drawn up and would help to keep the shoes on.
6. hide
7. (*d*) they were more comfortable, and easier to use
8. (*a*) employed ourselves in making; (*b*) various; (*c*) hog; (*d*) puckers; (*e*) succeeded in making
9. imperfect, passable, serviceable, nothing to boast of, useable, tolerable
10. active, busy, bustling, go-ahead, resourceful

II. 1. (*c*) a fire 2. (*b*) a pancake 3. (*a*) velvet 4. (*a*) a rake

III. horseback, newspaper, waistcoat, sandbank, honeymoon, railway

IV. 1. lost 2. will swim 3. clung 4. caught
5. will freeze 6. dived

V. 1. admirable 2. deceitful 3. imaginative 4. pitiful
5. talkative

Test 18

I. 1. fowling-piece, firelock
2. He thought that he had gone after a squirrel or a partridge.
3. He whistled and he shouted.
4. in vain
5. Flying about happily high in the air, above a tree.
6. (*c*) He was not able to move about as easily as before.
7. re-echoed
8. (*a*) precipice; (*b*) encrusted with rust; (*c*) turned his steps homeward
9. Rip's dog Wolf, a squirrel, a partridge, crows
10. (Individual answers)
11. complete

II. 1. a herd of cattle 2. a pack of wolves
3. a litter of puppies 4. a troop of monkeys

III. 1. The glasses lay in the boxes.
2. The armies cheered the chiefs.
3. The knights wore the coats-of-mail.
4. The potatoes were cut in halves.
5. The geese chased the mice.
6. The oxen drew the ploughs.

IV. 1. reside 2. excites 3. kneel 4. prove 5. gilds

V. 1. blacksmith 2. bus conductor (ticket inspector)
3. coal-miner 4. surgeon 5. conductor
6. navigator of a ship or aeroplane, or surveyor

Test 19

I. 1. It was started by pressing a button.
2. It was meant to travel into outer space.
3. They were all planets.

4. medicines (drugs); ammunition
5. (*b*) They were fearless.
6. (*a*) shiny; (*b*) transparent; (*c*) venture; (*d*) voyagers; (*e*) provisions; (*f*) necessities
7. (*c*) They had given up much of their time and pleasure.
8. (*b*) An Important Experiment
9. new, novel, recent, fresh, modern, up-to-date, brand, new, supersonic

II. 1. Have you begun your homework?
2. They taught him nothing at school.
3. "Your share is the bigger of the two," said Jo to Meg.
4. His pen is different from mine.

III. 1. perfume (scent) 2. librarian 3. harpoons
4. deciduous 5. decided (resolved)

IV. 1. Antarctic 2. vertically 3. lender
4. superior 5. temporary

V. 1. William; Anno Domini; Before Christ
2. Number; Street; Prime Minister; Member of Parliament
3. General Post Office; Station; British Railways
4. Colonel; Distinguished Service Order; United States of America; United Kingdom

Test 20

I. 1. tropical, sultry, sunny, baking
2. It refers to castaways similar to Robinson Crusoe who might be building boats, as he did.
3. He had cockatoos and goats as companions.
4. (*a*) bazaar; (*b*) mosque; (*c*) minaret; (*d*) goods
5. miles about
6. There is much desert land in the east and sand from it is found even in the city gardens.
7. (*c*) Imaginative Journeyings
8. (*a*) far; (*b*) Western; (*c*) poor; (*d*) selling; (*e*) going
9. bracelets, necklaces, papyrus, statuettes, muscatels, almonds, rubies, pearls, scimitars, lances, cinnamon, olive-oil, scrolls, coronets, amber

II. 1. ruin 2. then 3. soul 4. easy

III. Sentences 2, 5, 4, 1, 3.

IV. 1. The waitress was my sister's daughter.
2. The mistress of the house became the duchess.
3. "You are a heroine," said the queen.
4. The hostess called the maidservant.

V. 1. "Do you prefer apples, oranges or peaches?"
2. "May I have an orange?" asked Ann.
3. "Don't throw the peel on to the floor!" her uncle exclaimed.
4. "I'm not likely," said Ann, "to do that."

Test 21

I. 1. He had made up his mind to pass the night there.
2. admired
3. (*c*) a large number of times
4. hams, tongues, flitches of bacon, beef
5. (*b*) chatting in a friendly manner
6. active, brisk, alert, prompt, spry, enterprising
7. (*a*) determined; (*b*) of spacious dimensions; (*c*) beaming; (*d*) entered; (*e*) well-scoured; (*f*) other viands; (*g*) suspended from
8. (*b*) Travellers were well cared for. (*c*) There was plenty of meat available. (*e*) It was a pleasure to enter.

II. 1. cement 2. big 3. Bobby Shafto
4. shout 5. Frances 6. nail

III. 1. air force 2. our 3. skin 4. pupil 5. scabbard

IV. 1. RHUBARB 2. SAUCER 3. TONGUE
4. DECEIVE 5. GAOL 6. PETROL

V. Bradford, Chelmsford, Chester, Chesterfield, Durham, Newhaven, Newport, Poole, Pudsey, Wellington, Wells, Yeovil

Test 22

I. 1. The music came fairly soon.
2. The decorations worn were ribbands and greens.
3. Their visit was a peaceful one.
4. A large number of villagers and peasants followed them.
5. They struck them together.
6. It took place before the Hall door.
7. There was a feast after the dance.

8. beer
9. The squire was the most important man.
10. peasants, villagers, rustics
11. (*a*) skirts; (*b*) peculiar (curious); (*c*) concluded
12. They took place at Christmas-time.

II. bellowed, lowed, neighed (whinnied), droning, chimed, clanking, patter

III. 1. active volcano; ear-splitting explosion; sharp razor; blood-thirsty pirate; well-trained athlete; magnificent palace
2. exciting adventure; well-worn path; intelligent pupil; aching tooth; tremendous excitement; screeching brakes

IV. 1. fish 2. a chemist (dispenser) 3. incubator
4. in an aeroplane 5. digging ditches, roadmaking, etc.
6. an astronomer

V. 1. (*b*) to be very boastful
2. (*a*) to have a quick nap
3. (*c*) to tell something that was a secret

Test 23

I. 1. They were made from goat's skin.
2. The flap was to keep off the sun and the rain.
3. He used thongs of goat's skin.
4. He had a saw and a hatchet.
5. There was powder in one and shot in the other.
6. The belt around his waist was broader.
7. It hung over his right shoulder.
8. He had no shoes or stockings.
9. unusual, quaint, odd, ill-dressed
10. (*a*) open-kneed breeches; (*b*) jacket ,
11. He carried powder and shot.
12. (*c*) His cap was of no particular shape. (*d*) He wore two belts.

II. 1. scent 2. grate 3. hoard 4. muscle

III. clerk, dark; Braille, pail; tongue, swung; suite, meet; gnome, home; cheque, peck

IV. 1. margin 2. dampness 3. marvellous
4. labour 5. blameless 6. understanding

V. advance, chance, Seine, train, Harry

Test 24

I. 1. It took place in the High Street at Dunford, in the County of Loamshire.
2. There were farm wagons in the street going to the market-place.
3. He was on point duty, directing the traffic.
4. farm wagons, motor-lorries, cars, motor-cycles, bicycles
5. They were able to get past the larger vehicles and make their way to the front of the queue.
6. Petrol fumes poisoned the air.
7. They were impatient because they had been held up.
8. ran bleating sorrowfully
9. (*c*) He decided to take some definite action.
10. The tail-board of the lorry had collapsed.
11. stream of traffic, queue
12. honking, shouts, bleating

II. 1. sacred 2. athletic 3. morning 4. skilful 5. valuable

III. 1. Summer days are very pleasant.
2. Before going to bed one undresses.
3. New brooms sweep clean.
4. Remember to bring your dinner on Monday.

IV. 1. PRAIRIE 2. PRAWN 3. PRANCE 4. PRANK
5. PRAISE 6. PRACTISE

V. 1. rifle 2. trap 3. pool 4. port 5. page

Test 25

I. 1. He was at Florés, in the Azores, which are islands in the Atlantic.
2. It brought news that Spanish ships were coming that way.
3. Lord Thomas Howard
4. There were six English ships, and fifty-three Spanish ships were expected.
5. He made up his mind to sail away before the Spanish ships arrived.
6. He decided to stay as a number of his men were lying sick ashore.

7. It means his ship was anchored.
8. To these Inquisition dogs and the devildoms of Spain.
9. There might have been pinnaces, galleons, barques and galleys.
10. (*a*) Just Before a Great Sea-Battle
11. (*a*) like a fluttered bird; (*b*) fly; (*c*) out of gear
12. Although you sail away now, you mean to do battle later.

II. 1. originate 2. part 3. boiling 4. direct
5. lengthy 6. agreeable

III. 1. a, an 2. an, a, an 3. an, An 4. an, a, an

IV. 1. is worth two in the bush 2. keeps the doctor away
3. of themselves 4. the most sound

V. 1. hut, cottage, house, mansion, castle
2. mouth-organ, bugle, trumpet, trombone, double-bass
3. streamlet, stream, river, sea, ocean
4. second, minute, hour, day, week

Test 26

I. 1. (*b*) rather carelessly
2. (*c*) where they had been sent, but were asleep
3. It sounded like a pistol shot.
4. (*a*) to keep concealed; (*b*) by sundown; (*c*) had need of a hundred eyes; (*d*) still plainly in our view; (*e*) from their neighbourhood
5. arduous, difficult, laborious, awkward, uphill work, troublesome, beset with difficulties, wearing
6. (*b*) There was hardly a breath of air.
7. (*a*) At Bay
8. (*a*) escape, evade, retreat, elude, get clear, to slip through one's fingers, fugitives, dodge, to run for one's life; (*b*) follow, pursue, chase, hunt, hound, trackers

II. 1. angry 2. precious 3. cordial 4. top

III. Piccadilly, India, Africa, Alaska, America, Australia, Dutch, French, Italians, Atlantic, Pacific, London, Liverpool, Hull

IV. 1. citrus fruits 2. crockery 3. females 4. prepositions

V. 1. SNIPE 2. PUFFIN 3. CANARY
4. VULTURE 5. FALCON 6. THRUSH

Test 27

I. 1. It was labelled in this way so that no one would suspect its value.
2. They are lighthouses and all lie off the Cornish coast.
3. More and more of England gradually became visible to those on board the ship.
4. Large vessels cannot go beyond London Bridge, which is comparatively low.
5. It was placed in the vaults of one of London's great banks.
6. He had to come aboard to bring the ship safely up the Thames.
7. We often refer to the river by this title—'Old Father Thames'.
8. (*a*) merchandise; (*b*) in the fullness of time; (*c*) passage
9. exciting, perilous, hazardous, fraught with danger
10. (*a*) 'In the pool' means 'in any pool'. (*b*) 'In The Pool' refers to the Thames between London Bridge and Tower Bridge.
11. (*a*) valueless; (*b*) outward bound
12. underground chamber or cellar; leap over something

II. Of all the pleasant ways to pass an afternoon,
Is in a pony chaise one sultry day in June,
To drive between the trees in Hyde Park round and round,
It brings a pleasant sense of ease in spinning o'er the ground.

III. 1. DREAM, DREAD, BREAD, BROAD, BROOD
2. SWEAR, SWEAT, SWEET, SLEET, FLEET

IV. 1. The boy who was ill was absent from school.
2. Martin fell off the wall which was not very high.
3. This is the man whose coat is torn.
4. Here comes the soldier of whom we have been speaking.
5. Can you see what I can see?

V. 1. LABORATORY 2. DICTIONARY 3. NECESSARY
4. DORMITORY 5. DEPOSITORY

Test 28

I. 1. It came from a well on the slopes of Ben Venue.
2. She had to guard the sluice-gates of the stream.
3. She should have taken care, to avoid the risk of flooding.
4. The slopes of the mountain overlooked the valley.
5. It was named after the maiden of whom the story is told.
6. They can be seen only at a certain spot.

7. tragic, calamitous, disastrous
8. (*a*) limpid, bubbling, tranquil, gentle, placid, beauteous
   (*b*) turbulent, overwhelming, torrential, furious, cascading
9. (*b*) Katrine neglected her duties.

II. 1. ostrich's, hen's 2. brooch's, woman's 3. actor's, ladies'
4. mongoose's, tree's 5. night's 6. knives', cousin's

III. 1. The pilot shouted: "The plane is on fire; there is great danger."
2. "How far is it to the railway station?" he asked.
3. "Bring your library book without fail," the Headmaster told him.
4. Mr. Jones asked Mr. Smith: "Is Mr. Evans coming to the concert?"

IV. 1. cream 4. mash
2. toast 5. bacon
3. onions 6. Yorkshire pudding

V. 1. catastrophe 2. physical 3. geography 4. camphor
5. sylph (nymph)

Test 29

I. 1. We are told that the galley was making chase.
2. It was two miles away.
3. They were on the first ship.
4. There were about forty oars and two hundred to two hundred and forty rowers.
5. They walked up and down a gangway between the rowers.
6. They were chained in case they should try to escape.
7. They thought that the rowers were not rowing hard enough.
8. He was angry at the cruel treatment of the slaves.
9. half-naked
10. It was armed with cannon.
11. The great shock would be when the galley came alongside them.
12. The kitchen of a ship is called a galley.
13. (*a*) starving; (*b*) terrible; (*c*) snouts

II. 1. tepee (wigwam) 4. chalet
2. caravan 5. igloo
3. monastery 6. nunnery (convent)

III. tavern, entertainment, painted, curtains, sanded, side, door, clear, tobacco, customers, seafaring

IV. bray, bleat, grunted, crow, gobbling, clang, drip, creak

V. 1. more delicate, most delicate 2. farther, farthest
3. more cautious, most cautious 4. heavier, heaviest

Test 30

I.
1. He had been a king.
2. He should have harvested rice with a sickle.
3. untidy, unkempt, dishevelled, slovenly.
4. His native land is the country in which he was born.
5. (*c*) wide, long, and superior to many other rivers
6. The land was sandy, and he was harvesting rice, which grows only in warm lands.
7. (*b*) merchants and pilgrims travelling together for safety
8. (*a*) matted; (*b*) the landscape of his dreams; (*c*) bare
9. visionary, imaginary, fanciful, dreamlike, shadowy
10. serf, slave, bondsman, vassal, captive

II. 1. youth 2. confusion 3. science 4. curiosity 5. fame

III. 1. with 2. amongst 3. against 4. from 5. between

IV. 1. a pilot (a driver) 2. a bishop 3. a mechanic
4. an astronomer (seaman, coastguard)

V.
1. **biannual**—twice each year; **bivalve**—a shellfish with two halves to its shell; **bisect**—to cut in two
2. **Vice-Captain**—one who takes the captain's place; **Vice-Chairman**—one who takes the chairman's place; **Vice-Admiral**—one who takes the admiral's place
3. **pre-war**—that happened before a particular war; **prehistoric**—that happened before history was written; **predict**—to tell that something is going to happen
4. **postscript**—some writing added to a letter after the signature; **post-war**—that happened after a particular war; **post mortem**—an examination made after death

9. From this list choose words that describe the speaker: weak, enormous, puny, gigantic, tremendous, huge, microscopic.
10. Which of these titles describes the story: (*a*) Hurry and Bustle in the City. (*b*) An Unhappy Spectator. (*c*) A Rural Scene?

II. From the noun **care** we can make the adjective **careful.**

Make an adjective from the noun in front of each of the following sentences, and use it to fill the space.

1.	**adventure**	Martin was of an —— nature.
2.	**sorrow**	It was a —— time for all.
3.	**south**	The ship sailed in a —— direction.
4.	**giant**	You are planning a —— enterprise.
5.	**circle**	Your diagram should be ——, not square.

III. Rewrite the sentences below, filling each space with the correct word from this list: **with, from, in, to, of.**

1. I shall write —— the editor.
2. She takes pride —— her work.
3. I cannot agree —— John's answer.
4. Your reason is different —— mine.
5. He is jealous —— my success.

IV. From what type of shop or store would I buy the following?

1. tea, flour, sugar
2. plaice, herring, kippers
3. pens, ink, notepaper
4. apples, potatoes, pears
5. toffee, fudge, jellies
6. screws, saws, paint

V. Look at this: (**river, stream, brook**)—(mountain, **tributary,** dale). Of the three words in the second bracket, the word **tributary** is nearest in meaning to the three words in the first bracket.

Now do the same with these:

1. (boy, man, uncle)—(girl, nephew, lady)
2. (carrot, parsnip, beetroot)—(radish, pea, bean)
3. (peach, plum, cherry)—(apricot, apple, pear)
4. (wicked, bad, naughty)—(huge, great, evil)
5. (green, blue, red)—(yellow, black, white)

TEST 16

I. Read very carefully through the following passage, and then answer the questions.

Alan and David in the Mountains

We slept in the cave, making a bed of heather bushes, and covering ourselves with Alan's greatcoat. There was a low, concealed place in a turning of the glen, where we were so bold as to make a fire so that we could warm ourselves when the clouds set in, and cook hot porridge, and grill the little trout that we caught with our hands under the stones and overhanging bushes of the burn. This was indeed our chief pleasure and business, if only to save our meal against worse times. We spent a great deal of our days at the water's edge, stripped to the waist, groping about, or guddling, for these fish. The largest we got might have been a quarter of a pound, but they were of good flesh and flavour, and when broiled lacked only a little salt to be delicious.

R. L. Stevenson

1. Where did Alan and David sleep that night?
2. What did they use (*a*) for a bed; (*b*) to keep themselves warm?
3. Why were they able to light a fire without being seen?
4. For what three reasons was the fire used?
5. What does the word **burn** mean in the phrase **overhanging bushes of the burn?**
6. What did they wish they had when they were eating the trout?
7. From this list, choose words that describe the trout: lusty, appetising, uneatable, offensive, huge, palatable, massive, immense, mighty, undersized, inconsiderable.
8. They needed the trout to **save our meal against worse times.** Does the word **meal** mean (*a*) breakfast, dinner, etc.; (*b*) strength and cunning; (*c*) the oats from which the porridge was made?
9. What word tells us that (*a*) they **enjoyed** catching the fish; (*b*) it was **necessary** to catch the fish?
10. What words or phrases in the story mean (*a*) valley; (*b*) when the day became cold; (*c*) fry on the fire?

11. How were the fish caught: (*a*) with rod and line; (*b*) with the hands; (*c*) with home-made nets?

II. From the verb **to free** the noun **freedom** can be made. Change the verb before each sentence into a noun, and use it to fill the space in that sentence.

1. **to know** What —— have you of the subject?
2. **to educate** You have neglected your ——.
3. **to grieve** The lady was full of —— at the loss of her bag.
4. **to neglect** The house showed signs of ——.
5. **to imitate** That stone is not real, but is an ——.

III. Rewrite these sentences in the **plural** form.

Example: The **girl** fed the **swan.** The **girls** fed the **swans.**

1. The sheep browsed alongside the house.
2. My son-in-law fired the cannon.
3. She seized the glowing splinter with the tongs.
4. He stalked the deer through the mountain pass.
5. The sheath knife gradually cut through the thong.
6. The carton contained tasty cheese.

V. Name these characters from fiction:

1. He never grew up.
2. A poor boy who was befriended by Nicholas Nickleby.
3. A man in Sherwood Forest who was far from little.
4. He asked for more.
5. He lived first with little people, then with giants.
6. They sailed away in a beautiful pea-green boat.

V. Look at this:

Country—France; **People**—French; **Language**—French

Now complete these lists:

Country	People	Language
1. Belgium	?	?
2. Finland	?	?
3. Turkey	?	?
4. Mexico	?	?

TEST 17

I. Read very carefully through the following passage, and then answer the questions.

Making Shoes

We employed ourselves in making various garments of cocoa-nut cloth, as those with which we had landed were very ragged. Peterkin succeeded in making shoes out of the skin of a hog. He first cut a piece of hide, of an oblong form, a few inches longer than his foot. This he soaked in water, and while it was wet, he sewed up one end of it, to form a rough imitation of that part of the heel of a shoe where the seam is. He bored holes round the edge of the skin, through which a tough line was passed. Into the sewed-up part he thrust his heel; then, drawing the string tight, the edges rose up and overlapped his foot. There were many ill-looking puckers, but we found them very serviceable. Jack came to prefer them to his long-boots.

R. M. Ballantyne

1. What things did the boys make in addition to shoes?
2. Why was it necessary to make these things?
3. Why had the piece of skin to be longer than Peterkin's foot?
4. Why did he soak the leather before beginning to sew up the end?
5. What was the purpose of the holes that he bored?
6. What word is used in the story for **the skin of a hog?**
7. Did Jack prefer the shoes to his long-boots because (*a*) they had been made by Peterkin; (*b*) they cost more; (*c*) they looked much smarter; (*d*) they were more comfortable, and easier to use?
8. What words or phrases in the story mean (*a*) worked at making; (*b*) several kinds; (*c*) pig; (*d*) wrinkles; (*e*) managed to make?
9. From this list, choose words or phrases to describe the shoes that Peterkin made: exquisite, matchless, imperfect, passable, perfect, superlative, serviceable, nothing to boast of, useable, faultless, first class, tolerable.

10. From this list of words and phrases, write down those which might describe the life on the island: active, busy, bustling, sluggish, unoccupied, go-ahead, inactive, uninteresting, laggard, unemployed, resourceful.

II. When we wish to say that someone or something is **cold,** we may say **as cold as ice.**

Choose the correct answers from these:

1. As hot as (*a*) a cake; (*b*) a wire; (*c*) a fire.
2. As flat as (*a*) a skeleton; (*b*) a pancake; (*c*) a plate.
3. As smooth as (*a*) velvet; (*b*) wood; (*c*) a pavement.
4. As thin as (*a*) a rake; (*b*) a fork; (*c*) a spade.

III. Here are two words, **play** and **ground.** From these we can make the compound word **playground.**

Make six new compound words from the following:

horse	paper	waist	bank	honey	way
rail	moon	sand	coat	back	news

IV. Before each sentence there is a verb. Write the correct form of the verb in the space in the sentence.

1. **lose** He has —— all his possessions.
2. **swim** He —— —— in the river tomorrow.
3. **cling** Yesterday, you —— to the rope's end.
4. **catch** You —— that cold after bathing on Tuesday.
5. **freeze** As it is very cold, the water —— —— quite soon.
6. **dive** He —— to the man's rescue, and saved him.

V. From the verb **to poison** the adjective **poisonous** can be made. Change the verb before each sentence into an adjective, and use it to fill the space in that sentence.

1. **to admire** You have done an —— thing.
2. **to deceive** Your behaviour has been most ——.
3. **to imagine** That is an —— drawing.
4. **to pity** You are a —— specimen.
5. **to talk** This is the most —— class in the school.

TEST 18

I. Read very carefully through the following passage, and then answer the questions.

Rip Van Winkle Wakes Up

Rip looked round for his gun, but in place of the clean well-oiled fowling-piece he had an old firelock lying by him, the barrel encrusted with rust, the lock falling off, the stock worm-eaten. Wolf, too, had disappeared, but he might have strayed away after a squirrel or a partridge. He whistled to him, and shouted his name, but all in vain; the echoes repeated his whistle and shout, but no dog was to be seen.

As he rose to walk, he found himself stiff in the joints and wanting in his usual activity. He again called and whistled after his dog but he was answered only by the cawing of a flock of idle crows sporting high in the air about a high tree that overhung a sunny precipice. He shook his head, shouldered his rusty firelock and turned his steps homeward.

Washington Irving

1. Name the two words used that mean **gun.**
2. What did Rip think had happened to his dog Wolf?
3. In what two ways did he try to get Wolf to return?
4. What two words tell us that this was useless?
5. Write in your own words **sporting high in the air about a high tree.**
6. **Wanting in his usual activity.** Does this mean: (*a*) He wanted to take part in exercises. (*b*) He carried on as usual. (*c*) He was not able to move about as easily as before?
7. **The echoes repeated his whistle** means **His whistles** ——. Complete this sentence.
8. What words or phrases mean (*a*) steep cliff; (*b*) with a thick layer of rust; (*c*) made his way to his home?
9. What living creatures, besides Rip himself, are mentioned in the story?
10. The words **lock, stock** and **barrel** are all parts of a gun. But

each word has a second meaning. Write a sentence using each word in another sense.

11. Mr. Jones sold his business **lock, stock and barrel.** Write one word for the phrase in heavy type.

II. When we speak of a number of **sheep** we say a **flock.** What words should be used when speaking of the following:

1. A number of cattle
2. A number of wolves
3. A number of puppies
4. A number of monkeys

III. Rewrite these sentences in **plural** form.

Example: The **man** rode the **horse.** The **men** rode the **horses.**

1. The glass lay in the box.
2. The army cheered the chief.
3. The knight wore the coat-of-mail.
4. The potato was cut in half.
5. The goose chased the mouse.
6. The ox drew the plough.

IV. Before each sentence is a **noun.** Write the correct form of the **verb** made from that noun in the space in the sentence.

1.	**residence**	Where will you —— when you reach London?
2.	**excitement**	Teasing the dog merely —— him.
3.	**knee**	When you see the queen, —— before her.
4.	**proof**	You will certainly have to —— your point.
5.	**gold**	The craftsman —— the model of the saint.

V. **Who uses What?**

1. Who works at an **anvil?**
2. Who uses a **ticket-punch?**
3. Who carries a **safety-lamp?**
4. Who uses a **lancet?**
5. Who uses a **baton?**
6. Who uses a **sextant?**

TEST 19

I. Read very carefully through the following passage, and then answer the questions.

Space-Ship

It was only a matter of minutes before the starting-button would be pressed, and the giant rocket would begin its trip into outer space, carrying with it the seven intrepid men who had worked so self-sacrificingly upon the venture. There was a last check-over of provisions and other necessities, although everything had been examined a hundred times before. On a shelf were the cartons of 'Awake' pellets, 'Strength' tablets, and 'Sight' pills. In a cupboard were the tins of 'Space' bullets, 'Flash' caps, and 'Spray' cartridges. The 'Presto' gas-cylinders were piled neatly, and the 'Atmosphere' suits with their shiny, transparent head-domes of unbreakable material hung from hooks within easy reach.

Somewhere in the vast distances lay Mars, Mercury, Pluto. What terrible dangers lay ahead before the expedition would return to earth, and the voyagers would again see their homes!

1. How was the rocket started?
2. To where was the rocket intended to travel?
3. What have Mars, Mercury and Pluto in common?
4. Write one word for **pellets, tablets and pills,** and one for **bullets, caps and cartridges.**
5. The men were **intrepid.** Does this mean: (*a*) They were all of the same nationality. (*b*) They were fearless. (*c*) They were being forced to make the journey?
6. What words or phrases in the story mean the same as (*a*) gleaming; (*b*) easily seen through; (*c*) undertaking; (*d*) travellers; (*e*) food; (*f*) things that are needed?
7. The men had worked **self-sacrificingly.** Does this mean: (*a*) They had worked grudgingly and selfishly. (*b*) They had had to be forced to get on with the job. (*c*) They had given up much of their time and pleasure?
8. Choose the most suitable title from: (*a*) A Life on the Ocean

Wave. (*b*) An Important Experiment. (*c*) A Trip on Shanks's Pony.

9. From these words and phrases, choose those that describe the ideas and happenings in the story: new, novel, antiquated, recent, ancient, out-of-date, fresh, modern, antediluvian, up-to-date, old as the hills, brand new, supersonic.

II. There are errors in each of the following sentences. Rewrite the sentences correctly:

1. Have you began your homework?
2. They learned him nothing at school.
3. "Your share is the biggest of the two," said Jo to Meg.
4. His pen is different to mine.

III. Rewrite these sentences using single words instead of the phrases in heavy type:

1. The **pleasant smell** of the flowers was wafted on the breeze.
2. John asked the advice of the **man in charge of the library.**
3. The whale was struck by a number of **barbed, spear-like weapons.**
4. The oak and the ash are **trees that shed their leaves in winter.**
5. The centre-forward **made up his mind** to burst through alone.

IV. The opposite of **in** is **out.** Write these sentences, using the opposite of the word in heavy type to fill each space:

1. Nansen sailed to the **Arctic,** Scott to the ——.
2. The rocket moved off **horizontally** instead of ——.
3. "Neither a **borrower** nor a —— be," said Shakespeare.
4. Your work is **inferior**: Sally's is much ——.
5. The mansion was a **permanent** home, but the caravan was a —— one.

V. Write in full the **abbreviations** in heavy type in these sentences:

1. **Wm.** the Conqueror landed in 1066. Was that **A.D.** or **B.C.?**
2. At **No.** 10 Downing **St.** the **P.M.** spoke to the **M.P.**
3. The **G.P.O.** van took the letters to Euston **Stn.** for **B.R.** to move.
4. **Col.** Grant, **D.S.O.** sailed to the **U.S.A.** from the **U.K.**

TEST 20

I. Read very carefully through the following verse, and then answer the questions.

Travel

I should like to rise and go
Where the golden apples grow;
Where below another sky
Parrot islands anchored lie,
And, watched by cockatoos and goats,
Lonely Crusoes building boats;
Where in sunshine reaching out
Eastern cities, miles about,
Are with mosque and minaret
Among sandy gardens set,
And the rich goods from near and far
Hang for sale in the bazaar.

R. L. Stevenson

1. From this list choose words that describe the lands: tropical, Arctic, Antarctic, sultry, frigid, bleak, raw, sunny, frost-bitten, baking.
2. What is the meaning of the line **Lonely Crusoes building boats?**
3. What companions did the lonely boat-builder have?
4. What words or phrases in the story mean (*a*) market-place; (*b*) temple; (*c*) spire; (*d*) merchandise?
5. What words in the poem tell us that the Eastern cities were very large?
6. Why were the gardens of these Eastern cities likely to be sandy?
7. From these titles choose the most suitable for the poem you have read: (*a*) Dry-as-dust Existence. (*b*) Monotonous Occupations. (*c*) Imaginative Journeyings.
8. Finish these word-doubles suggested by the story: (*a*) near and ——; (*b*) Eastern and ——; (*c*) rich and ——; (*d*) buying and ——; (*e*) coming and ——.

9. Write down the things that would be for sale in the bazaars of the time to which the poem refers: wireless sets, bracelets, motor-cars, necklaces, valves, papyrus, statuettes, muscatels, almonds, cameras, rubies, pearls, tyres, gramophones, scimitars, lances, cinnamon, olive-oil, scrolls, oil-stoves, coronets, wrist-watches, fountain pens, amber.

II. We call **in and out** a word-double. Complete these sentences with the correct word-doubles.

1. Things are going to **rack and** —— at the castle.
2. **There and** —— the ship disappeared from view.
3. We must work **body and** —— to avoid disaster.
4. Things are far too **free and** —— at the camp.

III. Here are five sentences from a paragraph, but they are not in the correct order. Rewrite them in the order in which they should appear:

1. Would it enter the net?
2. Tom dribbled swiftly from his own half of the field, and shot.
3. Alas! The ball struck the upright and rebounded.
4. The ball curved past his clutching fingers.
5. The goalkeeper dived in an effort to save.

IV. In the following sentences, change all the **masculine** words into **feminine** words.

Example: **Mr.** Smith is my **father.** **Mrs.** Smith is my **mother.**

1. The waiter was my brother's son.
2. The master of the house became the duke.
3. "You are a hero," said the king.
4. The host called the manservant.

V. **Punctuation marks** and **capital letters** have been omitted from the following sentences. Rewrite the sentences correctly:

1. do you prefer apples oranges or peaches
2. may i have an orange asked ann
3. dont throw the peel on to the floor her uncle exclaimed
4. im not likely said ann to do that

TEST 21

I. Read very carefully through the following passage, and then answer the questions.

An English Inn

In the evening we reached a village where I had determined to pass the night. As we drove into the great gateway of the inn, I saw on one side the light of a rousing kitchen fire beaming through a window. I entered, and admired for the hundredth time, that picture of neatness and enjoyment, the kitchen of an English inn. It was of spacious dimensions, hung round with copper and tin vessels highly polished. Hams, tongues, and flitches of bacon were suspended from the ceiling. A clock ticked in the corner. A well-scoured deal table extended along one side of the kitchen, with a cold round of beef and other viands on it. Two housemaids were hurrying backwards and forwards, under the gaze of a bustling landlady. Travellers sat gossiping and smoking over their ale.

Washington Irving

1. How do we know that the writer knew of this village, and did not come upon it by accident?
2. Which word tells us that he was pleased with what he saw?
3. What does he really mean when he says **for the hundredth time:** (*a*) actually a hundred times; (*b*) what a hundred people had told him; (*c*) a large number of times?
4. What eatables are named in the passage?
5. What were the travellers doing besides smoking? Were they (*a*) playing draughts or dominoes; (*b*) chatting in a friendly manner; (*c*) quarrelling over who should pay?
6. From this list, choose words that describe the bustling landlady: active, brisk, sluggish, listless, alert, prompt, spry, lazy, unoccupied, drowsy, dormant, enterprising.
7. What words or phrases in the story mean (*a*) made up my mind; (*b*) roomy; (*c*) shining; (*d*) went in; (*e*) carefully scrubbed; (*f*) other articles of food; (*g*) hanging from?

8. Write down the statements that are true: (*a*) The inn was ill-lit and badly kept. (*b*) Travellers were well cared for. (*c*) There was plenty of meat available. (*d*) A single servant loitered about. (*e*) It was a pleasure to enter.

II. In each of the following lists, one item is out of place because it has nothing to do with the other four. Write down that item.

1. coal, coke, cement, peat, anthracite
2. big, in, from, out, to
3. Treasure Island, The Water Babies, Kidnapped, Bobby Shafto, Peter Pan
4. you'll, we'll, shout, shan't, don't
5. Peter, Eric, William, Cecil, Frances
6. saw, hammer, chisel, nail, plane

III. Complete the following:

Example: **Boy** is to **girl** as **man** is to ——. Answer—**woman.**

1. **Soldier** is to **army** as **airman** is to ——.
2. **I** is to **we** as **my** is to ——.
3. **Peel** is to **orange** as —— is to **banana.**
4. **Doctor** is to **patient** as **teacher** is to ——.
5. **Knife** is to **sheath** as **sword** is to ——.

IV. Here are some **crossword-puzzle clues,** and a part of each answer:

1. Sometimes eaten with custard.	R-UB-RB
2. Holds a cup.	S---ER
3. We use this when we speak.	T-N--E
4. To be false, or to cheat.	DEC--VE
5. Prison.	G--L
6. Fuel for a car.	-E-R-L

V. Write these names of towns in **alphabetical order:**

Yeovil	Wells	Wellington	Bradford
Chesterfield	Chester	Newhaven	Poole
Newport	Durham	Pudsey	Chelmsford

TEST 22

I. Read very carefully through the following passage, and then answer the questions.

Village Life

We had not been long home when the sound of music was heard from a distance. A band of village lads, without coats, their shirtsleeves fancifully tied with ribbands, their hats decorated with greens, and clubs in their hands, were seen advancing up the avenue, followed by a large number of villagers and peasants. They stopped before the Hall door, when the music struck up a peculiar air, and the lads performed a curious dance, advancing, retreating, and striking their clubs together, keeping exact time to the music; while one, crowned with a fox's skin, the tail of which hung down his back, kept capering round the skirts of the dance, rattling a Christmas box, with many antics. After the dance was concluded, the whole party was entertained with brawn and beef, and home-brewed. The squire himself mixed with the rustics.

Washington Irving

1. Did the sound of the music come immediately, fairly soon, or after a long time?
2. What decorations were worn by the young men?
3. Were they on a warlike expedition, or was their visit a peaceful one?
4. Who were following the young men?
5. What did the dancers do with their clubs?
6. Where did the dancing take place?
7. What happened after it was over?
8. What word has been left out after **home-brewed?**
9. Who was the most important man in the village?
10. Three words in the story mean **country people.** What are they?
11. What words or phrases in the story mean (*a*) edge of the dance; (*b*) unusual; (*c*) ended?
12. In what season of the year did the events take place?

II. Fill the spaces in the following paragraph with suitable **sound-words**:

Mary wandered through the farmyard. The bull —— in the field, and the cow —— in answer. Her favourite horse ——. A bee went —— homewards. Over the stable a clock ——, and the —— of chains showed that work was beginning. Rain began to —— as Mary went inside.

III. 1. Here are six **adjectives:** active, ear-splitting, sharp, bloodthirsty, well-trained, magnificent. Choose the most suitable to go with each of these **nouns:** athlete, razor, pirate, explosion, palace, volcano.
2. Here are six **nouns**: adventure, path, pupil, tooth, excitement, brakes. Choose the most suitable to go with each of these **adjectives:** aching, screeching, intelligent, exciting, well-worn, tremendous.

IV. Write down the answers to the following questions:

1. What would you expect to find in a creel: people dancing, cotton, fish, or salt and pepper?
2. Who would deal with a prescription?
3. What is a place called where chickens are hatched artificially?
4. If you heard someone say "Fasten your safety belts, please", where would you be?
5. What is the occupation of a navvy?
6. What do we call a person who studies the stars?

V. Here are some **everyday expressions.** Choose the phrase that means nearly the same as the everyday expression. Example: 'To lead a dog's life' means 'to have a most miserable life'.

1. 'To **blow one's own trumpet**' means (*a*) to play in a band; (*b*) to be very boastful; (*c*) to learn to play an instrument.
2. 'To **take forty winks**' means (*a*) to have a quick nap; (*b*) to be winking at someone for a long period; (*c*) to score points in a game.
3. 'To **let the cat out of the bag**' means (*a*) to release a cat from its prison; (*b*) to drive a cat out of the garden; (*c*) to tell something that was a secret.

TEST 23

I. Read very carefully through the following passage, and then answer the questions.

Robinson Crusoe's Dress

I had a great, shapeless cap, made of a goat's skin, with a flap hanging down behind to keep the sun from me, and to shoot the rain off from running down my neck. I had a short jacket of goat's skin, and a pair of open-kneed breeches of the same. Stockings and shoes I had none. I had a broad belt of goat's skin dried, which I drew together with thongs of the same, instead of buckles. On either side of this, instead of a sword and a dagger, hung a little saw and a hatchet.

I had another belt, not so broad, fastened in the same manner, which hung over my shoulder; at the end of it, under my left arm, hung two pouches, both made of goat's skin, too. In one of these hung my powder, in the other my shot.

Daniel Defoe

1. From what material were Robinson Crusoe's garments made?
2. Why did the cap have a flap hanging down the back?
3. What did he use instead of a buckle for his belt?
4. What took the place of a sword and a dagger?
5. What was in the pouches hanging from the second belt?
6. Which belt was the broader, that round his waist, or that over his shoulder?
7. Did the second belt hang from his right shoulder, or his left?
8. What garments was he not wearing, according to the story?
9. From these words, choose those that are true of his appearance: smart, unusual, stylish, quaint, odd, elegant, ill-dressed.
10. What words or phrases mean (*a*) short trousers; (*b*) coat?
11. How do we know that he had firearms?
12. Write down the statements that are true: (*a*) Crusoe's coat almost touched the ground. (*b*) The belt-buckle was made of brass. (*c*) His cap was of no particular shape. (*d*) He wore two belts.

II. Some words have a similar sound but are spelt differently. Example: **sale, sail.**

In these sentences, choose the correct word from those in the brackets.

1. The **(sent, scent)** of the pines was pleasant.
2. A log fire burned in the **(great, grate).**
3. The searchers found the **(hoard, horde)** of gold.
4. The runner strained a leg **(mussel, muscle).**

III. **He** and **me** are rhyming words. Write these twelve words in pairs, so that they rhyme:

clerk	Braille	tongue	suite	gnome	cheque
meet	home	peck	dark	pail	swung

IV. Look at this word—**shout.** Now look at the three words inside the bracket—(whisper, **yell,** murmur). The word nearest in meaning to shout is **yell,** so we choose that.

Now do the same with these, choosing one word from inside the bracket each time:

1. **edge** (centre, margin, middle)
2. **moisture** (dampness, drought, dryness)
3. **wonderful** (commonplace, ordinary, marvellous)
4. **exertion** (labour, relaxation, leisure)
5. **innocent** (sinful, blameless, guilty)
6. **knowing** (unaware, ignorant, understanding)

V. Choose, from the words in brackets, the most suitable word to finish the line of poetry:

Fair stood the wind for France,
When we our sails **(hoist, advance, release),**
Nor now to prove our **(vow, thought, chance),**
Longer will tarry;
But putting to the main,
At Caux, the mouth of **(Thames, Seine, Rhône),**
With all his martial **(train, band, army)**
Landed King **(James, William, Harry).**

TEST 24

I. Read very carefully through the following passage, and then answer the questions.

Trouble at Dunford

The High Street of the little town of Dunford in the County of Loamshire was more crowded than it had ever been. The policeman on point duty was having difficulty in directing the streams of traffic. There were farm wagons loaded with produce making their way towards the market-place, motor-lorries and cars. One or two impatient motor-cycles and bicycles edged their way towards the front of the long line of waiting vehicles. The honking of horns and the shouts of drivers became louder and louder. The fumes of petrol poisoned the air.

At this moment the tail-board of a lorry at the front of the queue collapsed. One by one, a flock of sheep scrambled down into the roadway and ran bleating sorrowfully to find a place of safety. The driver left his lorry and gave chase.

1. Where did the incident take place? Give full details.
2. How do we know that Dunford is a country town?
3. What was the policeman doing at the time?
4. Five types of vehicles are mentioned. What are they?
5. Why were the motor-cyclists and cyclists better off than the others?
6. Why did the atmosphere become unpleasant as time went on?
7. Why were the drivers impatient?
8. What phrase tells us that though the sheep were freed they were still unhappy?
9. Choose the statement about the lorry driver that is correct: (*a*) He remained impassive. (*b*) He contented himself with looking at the sheep. (*c*) He decided to take some definite action. (*d*) He realised that it was none of his business.
10. Why had the sheep been able to escape?
11. Two other words or phrases are used to mean **the line of traffic.** What are they?
12. Write down all the **sound-words** in the passage.

II. Think about the word FIRE. A **fire** need not be of **coal,** or of **electricity,** but it must be **hot.**

Choose one word from those in brackets that always has to do with the word before the bracket:

1. **church** (stone, large, sacred)
2. **footballer** (young, athletic, famous)
3. **breakfast** (plentiful, morning, expensive)
4. **doctor** (qualified, British, elderly)
5. **diamond** (necklace, valuable, smuggled)

III. The words in each of the following are in wrong order. Rearrange them to make sentences. (There may be more than one answer.)

1. Days summer very pleasant are.
2. Undresses bed before to one going.
3. Sweep brooms clean new.
4. Your Monday remember dinner to on bring.

IV. Complete these words beginning with PRA:

1. Grassy plain in North America.	PRA----
2. Small sea creature.	PRA--
3. To dance about.	PRA---
4. Practical joke.	PRA--
5. To commend.	PRA---
6. To keep on trying.	PRA-----

V. The word **game** has more than one meaning. It means 'something at which we play', 'birds like pheasant and partridge', and 'brave or plucky'. Write down the words that fit in with the following descriptions:

1. A weapon that fires bullets; to rob or plunder.
2. To catch someone or something; a horse-drawn vehicle.
3. A small pond; to share something.
4. A harbour; the left-hand side at sea; a drink.
5. Part of a book; an attendant at a wedding, or of a knight.

TEST 25

I. Read very carefully through the following verses, and then answer the questions.

The Last Fight of 'The Revenge'

At Florés in the Azores Sir Richard Grenville lay,
And a pinnace, like a fluttered bird, came flying from far away:
"Spanish ships of war at sea! We have sighted fifty-three!"
Then sware Lord Thomas Howard: "'Fore God I am no coward;
But I cannot meet them here, for my ships are out of gear,
And the half my men are sick. I must fly, but follow quick.
We are six ships of the line; can we fight with fifty-three?"

Then spake Sir Richard Grenville: "I know you are no coward;
You fly them for a moment to fight with them again.
But I've ninety men and more that are lying sick ashore.
I should count myself the coward if I left them, my Lord Howard,
To these Inquisition dogs and the devildoms of Spain."

Alfred, Lord Tennyson

1. Where was Sir Richard Grenville at the time?
2. What message did the pinnace bring?
3. What other admiral is named in the poem?
4. How many English ships were there, and how many Spanish were expected?
5. What did the other admiral make up his mind to do?
6. Why did Sir Richard decide to stay?
7. Sir Richard Grenville **lay.** What does this mean?
8. Which line tells us that the English and the Spaniards were mortal enemies, and that English sailors would be cruelly treated if taken?
9. From what you have read, which of these vessels do you think might have been at Florés at the time of the story: aircraft-carrier, pinnace, motor-boat, galleon, barque, galley, liner, tramp, submarine.
10. Choose a suitable title from these: (*a*) Just Before a Great Sea-Battle. (*b*) Two Make up Their Minds to Face Danger. (*c*) Preparations for a Peaceful Conference.

11. What words or phrases in the story mean (*a*) fluttering; (*b*) run away from; (*c*) unfit for battle?
12. What did Sir Richard Grenville mean when he said: **You fly them for a moment, to fight with them again?**

II. Look at this:

(unsightly, unattractive, ugly)—(pretty, lovely, **mis-shapen**). Of the three words in the second bracket, the word **mis-shapen** is nearest in meaning to the three words in the first bracket.

In the same way, find the similar words in these:

1. (begin, commence, start)—(end, originate, terminate)
2. (piece, fragment, share)—(part, total, whole)
3. (hot, warm, glowing)—(chill, boiling, bleak)
4. (straight, unbent, uncurled)—(winding, curling, direct)
5. (roundabout, longwinded, rambling)—(lengthy, brief, concise)
6. (pleasant, attractive, dainty)—(awkward, clumsy, agreeable)

III. We speak of **a** mouse, **a** tree, but **an** elephant and **an** ant.

Write **a** or **an** in the spaces in the following sentences:

1. Have you —— sunshade? No, I have —— umbrella.
2. Give —— egg, —— fresh egg, —— emu's egg in exchange.
3. What —— exciting tale. —— heir to the throne has been found!
4. I want —— apple and —— pear, not —— orange.

IV. Complete these **proverbs,** or well-known sayings:

1. A bird in the hand —— —— —— —— —— ——.
2. An apple a day —— —— —— ——.
3. Listeners hear no good —— ——.
4. Empty vessels make —— —— ——.

V. Write these **in order of size,** beginning with the smallest:

1. cottage, mansion, house, hut, castle
2. double-bass, mouth-organ, trombone, bugle, trumpet
3. sea, ocean, streamlet, stream, river
4. minute, week, second, hour, day

TEST 26

I. Read very carefully through the following passage, and then answer the questions.

In Hiding

The soldiers, having searched this side of the valley after a fashion, now stood dozing at their posts or only kept a look-out along the banks of the river; so that, in this way, keeping down the valley and at the same time towards the mountains we drew steadily away from their neighbourhood. But the business was the most wearying I had ever taken part in. A man had need of a hundred eyes to keep concealed in that uneven country, within cry of so many and scattered sentries; for the afternoon was now so breathless that the rolling of a pebble sounded like a pistol shot and would start an echo among the hills and cliffs. By sundown we had made some distance, even by our slow rate of progress, though the sentry on the rock was still plainly in our view.

R. L. Stevenson

1. **After a fashion.** Does this mean (*a*) dressed in fashionable clothes; (*b*) rather carelessly; (*c*) taking great care?
2. The soldiers were **dozing at their posts.** Does this mean they were (*a*) waiting for the post to be delivered; (*b*) each leaning against a post; (*c*) where they had been sent, but were asleep?
3. What did the rolling of a pebble sound like?
4. What words or phrases in the story mean (*a*) to stay hidden; (*b*) by the time the sun was setting; (*c*) needed very good eyesight; (*d*) could still be seen clearly; (*e*) from where the soldiers were standing?
5. From this list, choose words or phrases that describe the journey: arduous, difficult, laborious, easy, plain-sailing, awkward, uphill work, child's play, troublesome, beset with difficulties, smooth, wearing.
6. **The afternoon was now so breathless** means: (*a*) It was almost the end of the afternoon. (*b*) There was hardly a breath of air. (*c*) The soldiers were fast asleep in the afternoon.

7. Which of these would make a suitable title: (*a*) At Bay. (*b*) Picnic in the Hills. (*c*) Deer-stalking in the Mountains?
8. Arrange the following words and phrases in two lists: (*a*) those to do with the men in hiding; (*b*) those to do with the soldiers. Escape, evade, retreat, follow, pursue, elude, get clear, chase, hunt, to slip through one's fingers, hound, fugitives, trackers, dodge, to run for one's life.

II. From the words inside the bracket in each sentence, write down the one word that is nearest in meaning to the word in front of the sentence.

Example: **slender.** The man was of (ample, broad, **slight**) build.

1. **wrathful** The (agreeable, angry, pleasant) servant came to them.
2. **valuable** The ornament was (ancient, precious, worthless).
3. **friendly** The man's voice was (cordial, hostile, warlike).
4. **summit** The treasure was at the (base, top, foot) of the hill.

III. Rewrite this paragraph using a **capital letter** at the beginning of each **proper noun:**

If we walk down piccadilly we see shops selling goods from many countries. There are jewels from india and africa, furs from alaska, foodstuffs from america and australia. The dutch, the french, the italians all send us produce. Great vessels carry goods across the atlantic and the pacific, and unloading goes on night and day at london, liverpool, hull and other ports.

IV. Gooseberries, figs, dates, bananas are all **fruits.** Write down one word for each of these groups:

1. grapefruit, orange, tangerine, lemon, mandarin
2. cup, saucer, plate, mug, dish
3. woman, girl, niece, aunt, lass
4. in, out, near, to, from

V. **Jumbled words.** Find the names of these birds:

1. PINSE	2. PUNIFF	3. AANCYR
4. LTVUUER	5. ALNCFO	6. HHRTSU

TEST 27

I. Read very carefully through the following passage, and then answer the questions.

The End of the Expedition

The precious cargo, labelled as ordinary merchandise, was safely tucked away in the hold of a steamer, and the party found itself homeward bound. In the fullness of time, first the Wolf and the Bishop, then the Longships and the Lizard winked their welcome. England rose slowly out of the sea.

When the pilot came aboard at Dungeness to take them safely up 'Old Father Thames', they knew that their passage was nearly over. It ended when the vessel cast anchor and came to rest in The Pool, just below London Bridge. The signal 'Finished with engines' spoke a message to the returned treasure-seekers. 'Finished with adventure', it said, and the message was sad.

A few hours later the treasure was safe in the vaults of one of London's great banks. It was all over. The weeks of planning and doing were things of the past.

1. Why was the precious cargo labelled as **ordinary merchandise?**
2. What are the Wolf, the Bishop, the Longships and the Lizard, and where are they seen?
3. Explain the sentence **England rose slowly out of the sea.**
4. Why did the voyage **have** to end at The Pool, below London Bridge?
5. Where was the treasure placed for safe keeping?
6. Why had the pilot come aboard at Dungeness?
7. Why are there inverted commas around 'Old Father Thames'?
8. What words or phrases in the story mean (*a*) cargo; (*b*) when the time came; (*c*) voyage?
9. From this list, choose words and phrases that describe the life the treasure-seekers had been living: exciting, humdrum, ordinary, perilous, placid, hazardous, serene, protected, fraught with danger.
10. What is the difference in meaning between these two statements: (*a*) The vessel was in the pool. (*b*) The vessel was in The Pool?

11. Write words or phrases opposite in meaning to (*a*) precious; (*b*) homeward bound.
12. The word **vault** has two meanings. Write them down.

II. Write down this passage as it should be written, in verse. Begin each line with a **capital letter:**

Of all the pleasant ways to pass an afternoon, is in a pony chaise one sultry day in June, to drive between the trees in Hyde Park round and round, it brings a pleasant sense of ease in spinning o'er the ground.

III. Beginning with the word GRATE, and changing only one letter at a time, we can make the word BRAVO, in this way: GRATE, GRAVE, BRAVE, BRAVO. We call this a **word ladder.**

Now do these:

1.	DREAM	2.	SWEAR
Fear	-----	Perspiration	-----
We eat this	-----	Having a taste like honey	-----
Wide	-----	Half rain, half snow	-----
	BROOD		FLEET

IV. Below are pairs of sentences. Join each pair by using one of the following words: **who, whose, whom, which, what.** You may have to rearrange the words in some cases.

1. The boy was ill. He was absent from school.
2. Martin fell off the wall. The wall was not very high.
3. This is the man. His coat is torn.
4. Here comes the soldier. We have been speaking about him.
5. Can you see it? I can see it.

V. Complete the words below either with ORY or ARY:

1. The scientists worked in the	LABORAT---
2. He looked up the words in a	DICTION---
3. Do whatever you think	NECESS---
4. The boys slept in a large	DORMIT---
5. They stored the furniture in a	DEPOSIT---

TEST 28

1. Read very carefully through the following passage, and then answer the questions.

Loch Katrine

If you row a boat far out on Loch Katrine and, at a certain spot, gaze down into the clear water, you will see the ruins of cottages, farms and churches. For what is now Loch Katrine was once a peaceful and lovely valley where dwelt a friendly, hard-working race of folk.

For their water supply these people depended on a limpid stream that bubbled from a well on the slopes of Ben Venue that overlooked the valley. But when the rain beat fiercely upon the mountain, then the stream would flow swiftly, and care was needed so that the waters would not rush too madly into the valley below.

It was the business of Katrine, a young and beautiful maiden, to watch the sluice-gates of the torrent, and so keep the villagers from harm.

1. Where did the people of the valley get their water from?
2. What was Katrine's special duty?
3. Why should Katrine have been very careful to do this job properly?
4. How do we know that Ben Venue was **above** a village?
5. After whom was the lake named?
6. Can you see the ruins of the village from every part of the lake?
7. From this list, choose words to describe the happenings that must have destroyed the village: tragic, calamitous, pleasing, gratifying, disastrous, gladdening.
8. Make two lists of words: (*a*) those that describe the stream during fine weather; (*b*) those that describe it after heavy rain. Choose your words from the following: limpid, bubbling, turbulent, overwhelming, tranquil, gentle, placid, torrential, furious, cascading, beauteous.

9. Which of these statements is likely to be true of the story: (*a*) They all lived happily and peacefully ever after. (*b*) Katrine neglected her duties. (*c*) Nothing happened to disturb their happiness?

II. Write out these sentences, putting the **apostrophe** in its correct place.

Example: It was the girls book. It was the girl's book.

1. An ostrichs egg is bigger than a hens.
2. The broochs pin pierced the womans hand.
3. The actors disguise puzzled the ladies companions.
4. The mongooses enemies hid amongst the trees (one) leaves.
5. It was all a midsummer nights dream.
6. The knives blades cut my cousins coat.

III. Change these sentences from **indirect speech** to **direct speech.**

Example: The girl said that she had lost the ball. The girl said: "I lost the ball."

1. The pilot shouted that the plane was on fire, and that there was great danger.
2. He asked how far it was to the railway station.
3. The headmaster told him to bring his library book without fail.
4. Mr. Jones asked Mr. Smith if Mr. Evans was coming to the concert.

IV. The word **fish** is often linked with the word **chips.**

Write down the words that often go with those printed below:

1. Strawberries and ——
2. Poached egg and ——
3. Sage and ——
4. Sausage and ——
5. Liver and ——
6. Roast beef and ——

V. The answer to each of the following clues has in it **ph**, that sounds as **f.**

1. A tragic happening.
2. Having to do with one's body.
3. The study of lands and seas.
4. A bitter, strong-smelling substance.
5. A fairy-like creature.

TEST 29

I. Read very carefully through the following passage, and then answer the questions.

The Chase

Soon they were two miles away, with the galley making chase. It was an ugly-looking craft, rowed by about forty oars, each manned by five or six slaves. Between the two long lines of rowers, the English could see the slave-masters with their whips in their hands, walking up and down a gangway. Cannon poked their ugly snouts through portholes.

As the galley neared, the English could plainly hear the crack of whips and the yells of the slaves, the roll and rattle of the oars, the curses of the drivers. Amyas's heart was filled with anger as he thought of the wretched creatures who were fastened like wild beasts to the oars of this terrible craft. There might be Englishmen amongst those half-naked, starving wretches. They were now within forty yards; another minute and the great shock would come.

Charles Kingsley

1. How do we know that it was the **galley** that was following?
2. How far away was it at the beginning of the story?
3. Were the **watchers** on the first or on the second ship?
4. About how many oars were in the galley, and about how many rowers altogether?
5. How was it that the slave-masters were able to reach the slaves on either side with their whips?
6. Why were the slaves chained to their oars?
7. Why do you think the masters were cursing the rowers?
8. Why was Amyas so angry?
9. What word tells us that the slaves had few clothes on?
10. With what was the galley armed?
11. What was **the great shock** that was about to come?
12. The word **galley** can mean the ship itself, or something on a ship. What is the second meaning?

13. What words in the passage mean (*a*) in need of food; (*b*) awful and frightening; (*c*) muzzles?

II. Name the homes of these people:

1. Red Indian	4. Swiss farmer or mountaineer
2. gipsy	5. Eskimo
3. monk	6. nun

III. Rewrite the paragraph below, using a word from the list given to fill each of the spaces:

tavern	seafaring	curtains	entertainment
customers	side	painted	sanded
door	clear	tobacco	

I found the —— in question. It was a bright enough little place of ——. The sign was newly ——, the windows had neat, red ——, the floor was cleanly——. There was a street on either ——, and an open —— on both, which made the large, low room pretty —— to see in, in spite of clouds of —— smoke. The —— were mostly —— men.

IV. Fill the spaces in the following paragraph with the required sound-words:

The —— of an ass woke Mary. Her pet lamb began to ——, and a pig —— in return. It was before cock- ——, but already a turkey was ——. In the smithy, the —— of an anvil, the —— of water, and the —— of a hinge showed that Ben was working.

V. Richard is **tall,** Alan is **taller,** but Teresa is the **tallest** of the three.

In the same way, fill in the spaces in the following sentences:

1. Sheila is **delicate,** Pauline is —— ——, but John is the —— ——.
2. Tom went **far,** Jim went ——, and Jack went the ——.
3. He is **cautious,** his brother is —— ——, but his mother is the —— ——.
4. Jack is **heavy,** Jill is —— and Joan is the ——.

TEST 30

I. Read very carefully through the following verses, and then answer the questions.

The Slave's Dream

Beside the ungathered rice he lay,
  His sickle in his hand;
His breast was bare, his matted hair,
  Was buried in the sand.
Again, in the mist and valley of sleep
  He saw his native land.

Wide through the landscape of his dreams
  The lordly Niger flowed;
Beneath the palm-trees on the plain
  Once more a king he strode,
And heard the tinkling caravans
  Descend the mountain road.

H. W. Longfellow

1. What had the slave been in his own land?
2. What crop should he have harvested, and with what tool?
3. From this list, choose words that describe his appearance as he lay there: untidy, elegant, spotless, unkempt, dishevelled, spruce, faultless, slovenly, immaculate, tidy, regal.
4. What was meant by **his native land?**
5. Why was the Niger called **lordly** because it was (*a*) owned by a lord; (*b*) discovered by a lord; (*c*) wide, long, and superior to many other rivers?
6. How do we know that it was a warm land in which he was a slave?
7. **The tinkling caravans.** Were these (*a*) gaily-painted gipsy houses on wheels; (*b*) merchants and pilgrims travelling together for safety; (*c*) covered wagons?
8. What words or phrases in the story mean (*a*) tangled up; (*b*) the picture he was dreaming; (*c*) uncovered?

9. Write down the words in this list that describe what was happening: visionary, imaginary, real, positive, fanciful, true, dreamlike, positive, shadowy.
10. Which of these words describe the sleeper: serf, slave, leader, head, commander, bondsman, vassal, captive?

II. From the adjective **heroic** the noun **hero** can be made. Change the adjective before each sentence into a noun, and use it to fill the space in that sentence.

1. **young** All too quickly our —— passes.
2. **confusing** The entry of the pirates caused complete ——.
3. **scientific** I cannot study ——; I shall take up painting.
4. **curious** In many places such a hat would be a ——.
5. **famous** He sought —— and fortune overseas.

III. Rewrite the sentences below, filling each space with the correct word from this list: **between, amongst, against, from, with.**

1. I shall be angry —— you if you go home.
2. Share this money —— Jane, Susan and Ann.
3. I shall fight —— this decision.
4. He dived —— the pier each day.
5. Share this —— Brian and Mary.

IV. **Who uses What?**

1. Who sits behind **controls?**
2. Who wears a **mitre?**
3. Who makes use of a **spanner?**
4. Who uses a **telescope?**

V. 1. **Bi** at the beginning of a word means **twice.** Explain the meaning of these words: biannual, bivalve, bisect.
2. **Vice** before a word means **instead of.** Explain the meaning of these words: Vice-Captain, Vice-Chairman, Vice-Admiral.
3. **Pre** in front of a word means **before.** Explain the meaning of these words: pre-war, prehistoric, predict.
4. **Post** in front of a word means **after,** or **since.** Explain the meaning of these words: postscript, post-war, post mortem.